Metamorphosis

Thanks Kim, for all your help in putting me in touch with IFS. Best wishes for your continued success! The work you do is vital. Patti

Metamorphosis

Patricia R. Reule

With an Introduction by Dr. Sharon Wilsnack
& a Foreword by Annette Scharath

FirstPublish, Inc.
Orlando, Florida

ISBN
1-929925-79-4

Library of Congress Cataloging in Publication Data
2001092448

Patricia R. Reule
With a Foreword by Annette Scharath & Introduction by Dr. Sharon Wilsnack
Metamorphosis

FIRSTPUBLISH, INC.
300 Sunport Lane
Orlando, FL 32809
407-240-1414
www.firstpublish.com

FirstPublish, Inc.
Orlando, Florida

Dedication

Dear Julie,

You once told me: "A writer must write to feel whole. I hope you rediscover yourself..." I did. Thank you for reminding me of the best place to look.

Love, "Auntie Barbra"

Foreward

We each have friends we have known intimately since childhood. We shared hopes, dreams, secrets and sorrows. Patti has been that person for me, since grade school. We shared the effect of alcoholism in our families, an unspoken component of our families. We shared school, Confirmation, choir, and slumber parties. We are of the generation of girls raised to be teachers and nurses. Patti the teacher, me the nurse. We would visit when I traveled to North Dakota.

Nearly 3 years ago my mother became withdrawn, and it was necessary for me as case manager, to try get her interested in her surroundings. Hence, a trip to North Dakota . For some reason it was so very important for me to connect with Patti that trip; you could say I was driven. When we did connect, Patti told me it had been quite a year. She nearly died! She told me her story, how alcohol had almost robbed her of her life. My friend?? Yes, indeed. We made a promise to see each other, and we did a few weeks later, when I returned. But we also wrote . She was the same Patti I knew growing up, but, somehow more at peace with herself, despite the drama in her life at that time.

This book is about her return to a normal life, without alcohol. You will sense her courage, strength, humor (yes, it is real) , her candor, and her desire to give back to others. She wants to help you, be it in becoming sober, or helping a friend or family member to become alcohol free.

The teacher comes out, but she does it by showing, not preaching. She wrote the book with love. She is living the life she wants. I am so very proud of her!

Enjoy her story, it is the truth. I know... I am her friend. Friends are honest about each other.

Annette Scharath, B.S.N., RN, CCM, Physician Health Partners

Acknowledgements

When writing a book such as this, acknowleding and thanking all who played a part in the process is vital. It is also nearly impossible. The problem: the acknowledgement might well become lengthier than the book itself. Nevertheless, I won't let that stop me from trying.

First of all, I'm most deeply indebted to my family, nuclear and extended. Together, they became the support system that I relied on during the first uncertain days, weeks and months after treatment. Knowing that cushion was there allowed me to find the courage within myself to move forward. The world is a far less frightening place if you have people to whom you can turn for comfort as I did. "Thank you" seems inadequate. Still, it comes from the fullness of my heart.

To my son, P. J. Reule, my love and admiration. His vision and creativity, exhibited in the design and illustration of the front cover, embody the true spirit of this work. It is further proof to me that "A picture is worth a 1000 words." Or, as in this case, 35,000.

To my friends and colleagues, old as well as new, I also extend my sincere thanks. How easy it would have been for them to walk away and get on with their own lives. They didn't. Through cards, notes, phone calls and personal visits, they made clear to me that while I was temporarily down, they didn't consider me out. How does one repay such gifts?

I also owe a special thank you to the staff at Altru Hospital. In helping me to become physically well, they provided me the where-with-all and consequently the incentive to heal mentally and spiritually.

To Dr. Sharon Wilsnack, whose generosity of spirit and invaluable insight and advice helped to make this work a reality, I give special thanks.

Finally, to women everywhere who confronted their demons and fought back and won, thank you. You were and continue to be an inspiration.

I end this tribute to all of you, with love and gratitude from my heart to yours.

P

Introduction

When I began studying alcohol problems as a graduate student at Harvard in the 1970s, nearly all that we knew about drinking behavior was about males — male social drinkers, male problem drinkers, male alcoholics, even male mice, rats, and goldfish in animal laboratory studies. At that time, only a handful of published studies about drinking behavior had included any special attention to women.

Fortunately, the situation has improved considerably since that time. Americans have awakened to the fact that men are not the only humans who drink alcohol and experience alcohol-related problems. Research on women's drinking has proliferated; a 1997 volume referenced more than 1500 scientific books, chapters, and articles about how gender influences the use and abuse of alcohol (Wilsnack & Wilsnack, 1997). Women suffering from the clinical alcohol disorders of alcohol abuse and alcohol dependence (formerly called "alcoholism") have become increasingly visible and have sought treatment in growing numbers. Current estimates from the National Institute on Alcohol Abuse and Alcoholism (NIAAA), part of the National Institutes of Health, are that approximately 4 million American women meet diagnostic criteria for alcohol abuse or dependence (Grant et al., 1994). Our own 20-year study of a national sample of U.S. women suggests that more than one in ten women age 21 and older — approximately 13 million American women — experience at least one drinking-related problem a year, such as driving while intoxicated, loss of a job, family or relationship problems, or accidents in their home.

Another welcome change is that many women who have experienced alcohol problems first-hand have written and talked about their experiences in books, in magazine articles, and on radio and television. These personal stories have helped to focus public attention on women's alcohol abuse, and have helped to reduce the stigma that historically has led many women to conceal such problems.

Patricia Reule's book <u>Metamorphosis</u> differs from most other books by recovering alcoholic women, in several important ways.

First, unlike the "celebrity" authors of many such books, Patti describes herself as an "ordinary" woman from a small city in the upper Midwest. A former high school teacher, she and her family did not have the extensive economic resources that have permitted some more high-profile and prominent alcoholic women to use a wealth of treatments to aid their recovery. Readers of this book will find that Patricia Reule is anything but "ordinary" in her strength, character, and wisdom, but her modest social circumstances and lifestyle make her story relevant and appealing for women from a wide range of social backgrounds.

Second, although Patti is familiar with theories and research about alcohol use and abuse, she is writing not for professionals, but for other women like herself and their families. This is a practical book, with numerous suggestions for how to cope with everything from the digestive problems of early sobriety to the challenges of social entertaining as a non-drinking hostess. Her advice is valuable not only for women who are experiencing or recovering from alcohol abuse, but also for their families and friends, who may gain new insight into the sometimes bewildering behavior of the alcoholic woman.

Some of Patti's best wisdom is about ways that humor can help women deal with challenges that confront them when they are trying to overcome their alcohol problems. Patti has gone through several experiences that would severely test the strength of any woman and her family, but she has survived and moved beyond these in part by drawing on her own sense of humor, to maintain some perspective when problems otherwise might seem overwhelming.

Throughout this book readers will appreciate not only Patti's remarkable ability to find humor in difficulties that might have discouraged her, but also her strong sense of hope and optimism about the future. She communicates this optimism directly, encouraging other women with alcohol-related problems to realize that they, like her, can overcome those problems and find new peace and serenity in their lives.

I have spent my professional career studying the alcohol problems that afflict women, but I am always inspired and more than a little awed by the women who have been able to overcome the ravages of alcohol abuse and dependence. Patricia Reule is such a woman. Her honesty, humor, and hope can encourage other women who are now struggling to overcome their dependence on alcohol, as well as the family and friends who care about them. I hope that many of these people will be able to read this short but important book.

Sharon C. Wilsnack, Ph.D.
Chester Fritz Distinguished Professor
University of North Dakota School of Medicine
and Health Sciences Grand Forks, North Dakota

Is anybody out there?

Dec. 27, 1997

I awakened this morning certain of only one thing. I'm in trouble. Huge trouble. Physical, mental and emotional. The kind from which few, if any, survive. I haven't had a drink in a couple of days. So, this is what it's like.

My soon-to-be ex-husband is going on a short trip. In spite of our problems, he's reluctant to leave me alone. Somehow, from where I have no idea, I find the means to assure him that I'm fine, and that he should go.

Alone. I barely make it to the bathroom. My legs no longer want to support me; it scares me like nothing else ever has. Nothing, not food or water will stay in me. I make it back to bed; the remainder of the day floats by in a series of blurred images. Real, or a product of my imagination, I cannot say. I suspect both.

Still later in the day, I finally acknowledged what I'd stuffed down for way too long. I needed help. Right now. Most of what transpired after that point is little more than horrifying images. It's more than enough. I've read the books and articles. I know what I'm going through. I know what others will see. It no longer matters. Fear, shame and embarrassment are overcome by one inescapable fact: I am afraid I will die, when I desperately want to live.

You see, I'd been in free-fall for such a long time afraid I'd never land. Now, with the ground rushing to meet me, I no longer wondered if I would ; instead, the greater question became, would I survive the crash? I picked up the phone and called my son. My options had run out, including denial.

Sober, not somber

I've started this book several times. In my head. It's taken twists and turns, as I tried to figure out exactly what I wanted to say. More important was the matter of how to say it. My message is one of hope. It is also practical. I'm a woman, wife, mother, grandmother, sister, daughter, friend; I'm also a recovering alcoholic. The key word here being recovering. This has been and continues to be a journey. A journey for which there was no map, or road signs to show me how to best navigate my new life. After reading numerous articles and books, including the Big Book, I realized that there was very little for the average female addict to consult. I think this book can do what other publications don't: Address the everyday issues and situations that the recovering female addict is going to encounter. I recognize that every human is different; every experience unique. There are some universals however that most, if not all, recovering women will come up against.

Recovery can be scary. Just when you least expect it, a nasty curve ball is going to come out of nowhere. One of life's rules is you can't stop it. Given that, you better have some damn good coping skills in your pocket – you'll need them. Also included is some realistic advice for family and friends of the addict. One of the things I've discovered is that along with patience and understanding, maintaining a sense of humor is essential. Laughter is one of the best tools anyone can use for living, recovering addict or not . Often it's the ability to laugh that will help keep you from going insane. I wish I'd paid closer attention to that a few years ago. I didn't then. I do now. It has helped to keep me from going insane a second time.

In December of 1997, just after Christmas, I found myself being rushed to the hospital. Sicker than anyone thought, than even I thought, my life hung in the balance for a couple of weeks. It wasn't cardiovascular, but it was every bit as deadly. It wasn't cancer, but at least as insidious. It was alcoholism. You may be thinking "There's nothing funny about that". You're right, of course. There's nothing remotely funny about alcoholism or any other addiction. Hold that thought. I'll get back to it in a minute.

The causes, or reasons for my own addiction number as many as the ounces of booze I poured into my body. I suspect that this is true for any alcoholic. Any reason will do. *Reasons* aren't important. How one ultimately copes is. What I came to understand, what every addict, with help comes to understand, is that there is no *valid* reason to rely on any substance, be it beer, wine, pills or chocolate chip cookies to "get you through the night". It seems so obvious, now. It wasn't to me before recovery. Sadly for some, that basic concept remains elusive - at least for now.

As I said earlier, in the first stages of my own recovery, I was unable to find anything that I could relate to, in any meaningful way. There were no articles or books written by someone like me, or for me - an ordinary person, who had fallen victim to the disease. Those that were out there, were of an academic nature, or written by celebrities. While I certainly admire and applaud anyone who is able to beat the devil at his own game, I found it somewhat difficult to relate to a lifestyle so fundamentally different from my own. Those written by healthcare professionals were not much more helpful. They didn't tell me what to expect, either from myself, or those around me. It is for those people like me, especially women, that I write this book. As I discovered on my own journey, there is humor to be found, even in the midst of this kind of tragedy. It is one way to approach life in sobriety. It helped me, and continues to help me as I travel along the continuum of recovery. It's my hope that it will help others. I experienced during the course of my treatment, several situations that could either have been treated as a comedy or as a tragedy. I chose to see humor where at first glance there appeared to be little or none. It proved to be a wise choice. It worked for me; I have every reason to believe that it could work for you, too.

One thing I noticed during my hospitalization, and after talking with medical and mental health professionals, is that all too often they confused being sober with being somber. They aren't synonymous. It has occurred to me that one has little or nothing to do with the other. As recovering alcoholics, we're seeking permanent sobriety, and towards that end will have to approach it seriously; not necessarily somberly. If there is one thing that recovering addicts do a lot of, it's crying. Before seeking sobriety and recovery, we were awash in denial. Not any longer. As recovering addicts we often find ourselves awash in tears. Those, like laughter, are healthy and necessary. I believe they're among the world's best cleansing agents. But there comes a point where the crying has to stop. Not because you might run out of tears - you won't. You need to get back the world of the living. There, most people don't spend their lives in tears. They might find it odd if you do.

In the hospital

It may seem strange, even redundant, discussing "hygiene in the hospital." Really it's not. It goes without saying that the hospital staff will do everything it can to ensure that you shower and/or bathe as often as you feel like it. But - what else can you expect?

For starters, you may have to rely on Depends, or some other adult diaper. And just so we're clear, that's what it is, a diaper. Not adult underwear. And they sure as hell, no matter how positive a spin you put on it, cannot be referred to as "lingerie". As in other areas of your life, you must learn to call a spade a spade.

There's a reason, indeed a need, for these garments. They're temporary for most people . Many alcoholics have extremely poor eating habits. Once the booze is out of your system, your appetite will return with a vengeance. This is a good thing. What isn't: your digestive system, deprived of decent nutrition for God only knows how long, may temporarily rebel at what it thinks is foreign matter. As a result, your gastro-intestinal tract happy to be back in business, begins to process whatever comes down the pike, so to speak. To a fare-thee-well. I'm no doctor, so I can't tell you exactly what is happening or why for certain, but it does happen. Picture it this way: That little "gas bubble" you think you're having isn't gas at all! Get my meaning? Sure you do. It's neither reasonable nor practical to expect to wear "regular" underpants at this time.

Understand that in all likelihood, it won't last forever. Consider it part of the process.

You may be wondering where the laughter is in any of this. First of all, if you don't see the humor in the concept of adult diapers, I doubt that you'll find humor in the rest of this. Think about it. We start out in life helpless, wearing diapers. For some, diapers will make an another appearance in adulthood. Not because we're helpless. What some do need for a brief (sorry) period of time, is one less thing to worry about. As recovering alcoholics, we have much weightier matters on our minds. The security provided by Depends, or items of a similar nature, helps to simplify our lives at a time when all things need to be reduced to their simplest form. As for giving up your dignity: Face it - you surrendered that at the door the last time you drank. Now, about those laughs I mentioned.

One morning, a chirpy little LPN showed up in my room after breakfast. "Are you ready to shower and get dressed?" she asked.

"Yes", I replied. Showering and dressing had become high points in my morning. After that, it was all downhill- or uphill depending on your viewpoint. Physical therapy was my other morning activity.

"Oh, darn. I have to go to the laundry closet to get your Depends. I'll be right back." And so she was, in a matter of minutes.

"I didn't know what to do. They're all out of small," she moaned. I was a trifle skinny at that point.

"That's OK", I replied. "I think I can make a medium work." Wear turtleneck, sweater, tuck them in.

"Oh, God! This is awful! All that's left is LARGE." Large happens to fit, well, large people. At that time I weighed 90 pounds. I'm sure you get the picture. Gamely, I told her to bring them on; I'd make them work. Meanwhile, I headed for the shower. When I finished, I came back to my room and found her waiting with my "undergarment". I should mention that I"d popped on a nightie after showering, just in case she wasn't back. I

stepped into them. Did I say they were large? Think para-
chute. I pulled them up, then quickly whipped my nightie
over my head. At the precise moment the nightie left my
body, so did my Depends. There I stood in seconds without
a stitch, my drawers drooping around my ankles. It was
funny and I began to giggle. That sweet LPN was horrified
to see what had happened on her watch. For some reason,
she felt responsible. Pulling myself together, I assured her
that neither my dignity nor my ego had suffered irreversible damage. I pulled up my "panties", pinned them on
the sides,(that diaper thing again!) and slipped into my
sweat pants.

One more thing about hygiene . You will know, better
than anyone else, when you need to use the bathroom - for
any reason. Be clear, be assertive and be doggoned sure
that you get to a bathroom when you need to, not when
they tell you it's OK.

One morning, again right after breakfast, a doctor and
a few nurses came in to palpate my abdomen. This will
happen a lot, as they're trying to determine the extent, if
any, of the liver damage you may have sustained. I was
about to ring for someone to help me anyway. I needed to
use the toilet. Desperately. When the medical team walked
in, I told them.

'OK. Just wait a few minutes. This won't take too long."

"I really need to go."

"Just hold on,(palpating while she spoke) just a little
longer." You're familiar with the expression "the s-t hit the
fan"? In this case, it hit the aide; spattered him, actually.
He shot me one hugely disgusted look, and left the room.
What? Like no one was warned? Was I embarrassed? For
myself, only marginally. For them, tremendously. As far as
I'm concerned, they violated a main principle of medical
care: The patient comes first. So, patient, speak up
already.

I'd be remiss if I didn't mention one episode, out of
many, that clearly underscores the kindness and compassion I also received, while a patient.

As I grew stronger I also, not surprisingly, became more active. With increased activity, came an increase in my appetite; no big surprise either. The problem, if it can be called that, stemmed from the fact that I wasn't able to eat much at one time. As a consequence of that, I was hungry often. Real often. For example, I awakened once around three in the morning. I'd had no trouble falling asleep or staying asleep before for that matter, so I was at first puzzled as to what it was that awakened me. Within a minute or two, I had it figured out: Hunger pains had brought me out of a deep sleep. I was ravenous. I was shocked at first. Never in my life, had hunger awakened me. I knew only one thing: I needed food - immediately. I rang for a nurse.

"Can't you sleep, Patti? Are you in pain?"
Embarrassed because there wasn't anything seriously wrong, and I didn't want to take her away from someone that really needed her, I nonetheless heard myself ask: "Do you have any crackers that I can snack on? I'm hungry." To my ears, I sounded self-indulgent, truly pathetic. There were sick people that need care, and I had the munchies! She didn't bat an eye. Instead, she asked: "How about if I make you some toast? Would you like that? Do you like peanut butter or jelly with it?"

My salivary glands kicked in. A seven-course meal wouldn't have sounded as good. "Yes, please. Both."

"Would you like milk or juice to go with the toast?"

"Milk, please." In short order, the toast and milk arrived. I have absolutely no memory of eating the toast or drinking the carton of milk, but I must have. Minutes later, the nurse came back to check on my progress. All that remained on the plate were a few crumbs. The milk carton was bone dry.

"Would you like some more?"

Feeling better and somewhat less embarrassed but still hungry, I said yes. In no time, she was back with more milk and toast. The second helping, I tasted. Altogether, four slices of toast with peanut butter and jelly; two cartons of milk. By the clock, fifteen minutes from the time she entered my room for the first time, until I polished off the second half of my snack. That may be some kind of record. I didn't care. Nothing I'd eaten before or, for that matter, since, has tasted quite so good as that middle of the night "break fast". By the way, seconds after she took the empty plate and milk carton away, I curled up and was fast asleep. Second childhood? Second infancy? Nope. My body called out for nourishment and I answered the call, with a little cooperation from another human being. At the tender age of 51, I was learning to take care of myself in a positive way. New, different, exciting. Also, satisfying. Rather than be a martyr and go hungry (and be miserable), I simply chose to speak up and ask for what I needed.

The most important point to all of this is: Be in charge of yourself, as much as is possible. For far too long as addicts, we abdicated personal responsibility in favor of oblivion. If you need to resort to Depends while you're getting back on track, do so without embarrassment.

Nocturnal feedings? So what? You don't want others to see you like this? Believe me, they've seen you look worse. Do what the medical professionals tell you to do, but make sure that they listen to you, too. You've taken the first step towards regaining control over your life, by choosing sobriety. Don't give up now. Only better days lie ahead.

Getting to know yourself

Hospitalized or not, one thing will become clear – you're probably going to need therapy. What kind and how much will vary of course, from one person to another. A phrase in vogue today is that alcoholics, drug addicts, etc., have "issues". That's a load! The truth is everyone has issues. Learning to cope with those issues is what separates the addicted from the not; and that's where therapy will help. Sooner or later, the issues will have to be dealt with - or, you can choose to ignore them and suffer a slow kind of suicide, because that is precisely what you're doing when you depend on artificial substances. You may not want to die - I didn't. Nonetheless, I was killing myself with every drink I took. That's a fact. If you're reading this, you've chosen already, so snap to it. Let me make one point abundantly clear: Talking about those things that have troubled you won't make them go away or make them more palatable. What it will do is make you better by showing you how to tap into the strength that has been there all along.

I'm reluctant to discuss drug therapy, for obvious reasons. For some of us, drugs, not booze were the original culprit. That being said, your doctor or therapist may recommend some type of anti-depressant, to help get you through the rough spots. I am not a specialist or a therapist, but I am a recovering alcoholic, and this much I do know: As addicts, our coping skills, such as they were, left much to be desired. Why substitute one drug for another? Like I said before, troubles will follow us no matter where we go. No time like the present to learn how to cope without artificial help. It was my experience, and after talking with other women I'm convinced: the medical profession is all too ready to dispense Prozac or Zoloft, to smooth life's rough edges. It seems to me that most people would be better off meeting it, acknowledging the obstacles, and dealing with them as best as is humanly possible. What does anyone gain by replacing booze with a pill? I didn't get it then and I don't now. Still, I'm in no position to judge; the final decision will be your's and your doctor's. One last thought before moving on: It would be irresponsible of me if I didn't acknowledge the reality of and the difference between, primary and secondary depression. There's a big difference. The depression that may result from alcohol abuse is generally considered to be secondary. It is to those individuals that I address my remarks. Others, who suffer from primary depression, i.e. that which is believed to be physiologically induced (chemical imbalance perhaps), have and will continue to benefit from the use of drug therapy to help them live productive lives. It's important to remember that each of us is a unique individual. Accordingly, each of us will learn to live healthy lives employing a variety of methods. Happily, there is no "one size fits all" treatment. You will come to learn which method is the most effective and healthiest for *you*.

Earlier on, I mentioned tears. There will be, count on it. You may say to yourself, I'm not a crier- never have been, never will be. That's another load! Were you hatched as a fully-grown adult? Of course not. You were a baby. Babies cry. Therefore, at some point in your life you cried. Trust me. As we grow and mature, we become culturally and sociologically conditioned to rein in our feelings. "And, for God's sake, don't be a crybaby!" Most people over the age of forty can remember hearing as children: "You better stop that crying, or I'll give you something to cry about."

As someone once reflected on *that* parental threat: I thought I already had something to cry about.

And so we grow and we repress and we become "good girls" and "big boys" and we put a lid on ourselves. But, one thing remains constant. Though life can be thrilling and exciting; it can also be cruel and disappointing. The lesson learned so well in childhood-don't let anyone see how you feel - becomes a part of the blueprint by which we direct our adult lives. So. During therapy, you may "revisit" some places you'd rather not. Don't worry about it. You don't have to visit too long, and you don't have to live there. Realize that, in spite of everything, you're still here. Whatever else may be true, and this is key: You're a survivor. Therapy will show you how to let go - hurts and all, and look forward. That's where your future is. That's where life is. It's really as simple as that. Besides showing you how to wield your own power, therapy can also help to show you who you truly are. Chances are, you were never really clear about that anyway. Word of caution here: As you get to know yourself,(and you will!) others, who "knew you" BS (Before Sobriety) may have difficulty recognizing the person they thought they knew. Don't worry about that either. You're not the same person. But, this is the person you were meant to be. Let others adjust. You have enough work ahead of you as it is.

Now, you may also have to undergo other kinds of therapy, specifically physical and occupational.

At first, I was mildly amused when told I'd need occupational therapy. They already knew I had given up teaching. (That was one of the sane things I did while still drinking. I was beginning to find less joy and more frustration in a career I'd once loved. It was time for a change.) So, I wondered, what occupation was I being rehabilitated to? Turns out, the only other occupation that I'd held my entire adult life - housewife! No kidding. I had to prove to them that I hadn't lost my ability to use the sink, stove, make the bed, set the table, or dress! While I do believe that booze kills brain cells, this seemed to me to be rather unnecessary. Nonetheless, keeping my goal in mind (getting out of there) I jumped through their hoops. Again, I can't stress enough - do what is required to keep you moving forward. That should not be your main focus, it should be your only focus. It's your *life*, so get on with it. Sometimes, the rules may seem silly.

For instance: One morning, I was told that I would have my "dressing test" the next day. I must have had an unusually vacant look on my face, because the O.T. went on to explain that I had to show her that I could pick out appropriate clothes to wear and put them on correctly. Was she kidding? The next morning after breakfast and a shower, not giving it a second thought, I walked to the dresser and pulled out my clothes for the day. Big mistake. I was supposed to wait for her, so that she could observe me choosing the clothes. She showed up just then, so I explained what I'd done. I offered, (tongue in cheek) to put everything back and do the whole thing over so that she could watch. I also offered to pick out something different so she'd know that there was no subterfuge afoot. She assured me, (quite seriously) that what I had done was all right, and I could proceed with part two of the test - dressing. What in the hell did she think I was going to do? Wear my tee-shirt as a headdress? My socks as mittens? Anyway, I dressed - apparently correctly, because she gave me a passing grade. One more thing. At first while you're in the hospital, you'll only wear a nightgown; one of theirs or one of your own. When you go to rehab, you'll be expected to dress. As a general rule, most people are so glad to reach that point that putting on real clothes is a treat, not a hardship. Strange as it may sound, it's one step closer to helping you realize your goal, which is feeling like a whole person, again. That said, you can within limits, determine what you will, or as in my own case, won't wear. Putting on a bra has always been, and continues to be for me, pretty much a waste of time and effort. When I was twelve, I begged and pleaded until I finally got one. All the girls in gym class had them. I didn't need one then. Nothing has changed. I informed my O.T. that unless threatened physically, I would not put one on. I'd be happy to demonstrate that I know what it is, and where it should go, (actually, I've got a couple of thoughts about that) but I categorically refused to harness myself. Maybe it was the slightly crazed look in my eye; (I was beginning to tire of their tests; I was also getting my "voice" back) she wisely decided to let me win that battle before things got ugly.

I wasn't so lucky in the kitchen. If you've been hanging around a kitchen as long as I have, you have your own way of doing things. It may not be the right way for everyone, but it works for you, so who cares what others think? I prepared lunch ; tuna salad sandwiches and chicken noodle soup. She gave me a strange look when I requested dill pickles. She relaxed when I explained that I always put diced pickles in every sandwich spread I make. This could have been a slippery slope, but it turned out all right.

I also "messed up" with the stove. After I dished up, I turned the burner under the soup to slow-simmer, just like always. That's where I made my mistake. Didn't I know about safety first? I don't mean to be sarcastic ,(OK, maybe a little) but I've been doing that for over thirty years, and haven't started a fire yet. I explained all that - it didn't make any difference. Lips pursed, she docked me a few points on my kitchen test. That was all right though. She might have docked me more if she'd read my mind.

No matter. Point is, I had a purpose. You have a purpose. We know what that is. To do that, you need to be well and demonstrate to others that you are well in mind, body and spirit. So, just do it - their way. When you get home, do it however the heck you want. It's your kitchen, isn't it?

While you may find O.T. occasionally annoying, you will find physical therapy grueling. Alcoholism and physical fitness are not bosom buddies. That's not opinion, it's a fact borne out of scientific research. Whether you find yourself in a hospital or not, you will find that some physical rebuilding is in order. In my own case, there was a lot of re-building to do. Without sounding like a hypocrite however, on occasion I found myself butting heads with the rehab staff - even before I began physical therapy. Early on, because of my weakened physical state, I wasn't allowed out of bed on my own. I had to ring for assistance even to take the few short steps to the bathroom. Well, we already know what happens when we don't reach the facility in time. Moreover, I was convinced in my own mind, that the more I tried to navigate on my own, the quicker I'd get back on my feet 100%. I had been raised in the belief that each of us is capable of doing more than what we originally think is possible. Apparently, the staff there had not. We had a small conflict. Not surprisingly, I wasn't particularly quick on my feet, so each time I made a solo attempt to get to the bathroom, someone always happened to be walking by. Busted.

"Patti, what are you doing out of bed?"

"I need to use the bathroom."

"You're supposed to ring for someone to help you. You're not strong enough to walk by yourself."

"I'm holding on, all the way." And I was. Someone had conveniently designed and set up the room, so that indeed I did have something to grab hold of: the adjacent bed, the dresser, the wall, the door casing; then, BINGO! home free and in the bathroom! This annoyed the staff particularly at night. "To catch a thief" in the night, they cleverly attached an alarm to my bed that would flash a light at the nurses' station, if I set so much as one toe on the floor. Thirty seconds was all the time it took me to disarm it. It became a sort of game: Up I'd get, caught I'd become, back to bed I'd go. Once, they found me in another patient's room. My bathroom was occupied, or so I thought. The door had simply been closed tight, and I thought it was in use. I needed to pee, and my neighbors in the next room were fast asleep. I was sure that they wouldn't mind. They didn't. The nurses did. I got written up that time. No matter. It didn't stop me. And so, our nightly "dance" continued. I wasn't their favorite patient. In all fairness, there were many times when I rang, and they did come running. One night, I was certain I'd heard a small child or infant crying. They assured me that neither a child nor a baby was anywhere on my floor. Quite obviously I'd been dreaming, and the "reality" of the dream caused me to awaken. Before I get to the more positive aspects of my rehab stay, there's one other item that needs mentioning.

Physical challenges weren't the only obstacles that I needed to overcome.

Both the hospital and the rehab staffs felt certain that I had suffered irreversible brain damage. Whether the result of trauma from withdrawal, or the overdose of drugs I'd been given upon admission to the hospital, is anybody's guess. When I was at my lowest ebb, and little hope was held out for my survival, one doctor determined that I had been far over-medicated, and that the key to my recovery and awakening lay in a sharp and immediate reduction in the amount of "stuff" being pumped into my body.

Within an incredibly short time period, I began my journey "back" although for reasons not clear, I was often confused, especially early on. So much so, that the medical team attending me had my family convinced that they needed to start looking at nursing homes for my long-term care. A word of caution here, for the families of others going through treatment: Confusion, I think, is natural. As the body rids itself of toxins of any kind, profound chemical changes are bound to occur. One of the odd things was, I knew that I was confused, and often expressed that confusion by giving the wrong date for example, but insisting that I was right. When someone would point out my error, I became angry. Often at myself. At other times, I was crystal clear in my head, and thought that they were out of theirs. Particularly when the tone they used when speaking directly to me was one I reserved for infants and not quite bright children. I don't really believe that their intent was to demean in any way. They had no way of knowing, initially, what my level of comprehension was. I decided to show them.

One day, very shortly after "waking up" and while visiting with my husband, I heard a voice at once familiar and dear to me.

"There's Judy," I said.

My family had been told that in all likelihood, I probably wouldn't recognize all of them when I *saw* them. I'd already disproved that. That day, I took it a step further and demonstrated that I could also recognize and identify one voice out of a cacophony of several, all going at the same time. As long as I'm in my "whining mode", (who hit *that* button, anyway?)I have one last event to relate.

I failed another of their "tests". It consisted of placing blocks into a predetermined pattern. Each was cut so that the angles had to line up just right, or the block puzzle wouldn't go together at all. I nearly failed geometry as a sophomore in high school. My math skills were no more impressive at 51 than they had been at 15. Nevertheless, I saw that the "proctor" wrote that I was unable to perform simple tasks and became frustrated very easily. Oh, yeah? There was nothing wrong with my "reading upside down" skills. I wondered how *she* was in that department. I was also given word problems to solve. I hate word problems. In eighth grade math class, I repeatedly failed to calculate correctly what time two trains would pass each other, one from Baltimore, the other from New York, if one was traveling 70 mph, and the other 80 mph. I really didn't care. Of far greater concern to me was that they not crash into each other. Failure at 13; failure again at 51. One more instance of my inability to problem-solve. Really? Give me a problem I think is worth solving. Then, we'll see.

Allrighty. Now that I have that off my chest, I can get back to the real purpose of this chapter: Physical therapy: Getting through.

There is an upside: When you're down as far as I was, there's only one way to go, and that's up. That's the upside of PT - the only one. I'm kidding, of course. But I'm not kidding when I say that it's damn hard work! I started from ground zero, sitting up in a wheel chair for 15 minutes at a time. What none of us appreciates, addict or not, is what a remarkable machine the human body is. Like a Timex watch, it really does "take a licking and keep on ticking!" Today, I do a daily workout, of at least 30 minutes, that includes 2 miles on a stationary bike (with ankle weights) in 10 minutes. Let me tell you how I got to here from there.

Physically, I was a wreck. I didn't get that way overnight, and I couldn't fix it overnight, either. Never in my life, including giving birth, have I expended as much energy as I did during my PT sessions. My motivation was simple: I HATED my wheelchair.

I'd enjoyed good health most of my life and been active, having danced for over twenty years. Suddenly, I was being propelled towards a wheelchair! With a nurse on either side of me, I was told to "walk" to what looked like a Laz-E-Boy on wheels, with a TV tray attached. No problem, I thought. I proceeded to stand up. Although I knew what I wanted to do, and I sent the appropriate message to my brain, the signal must have become scrambled; my legs refused to hold me up. The shock registered on my brain, unlike the recent command I'd given it . The legs I'd taken for granted, and made fun of (too short, too fat) were simply unable to do what my mind told them to do. I don't know why, but a scene from Gone with the Wind popped into my head. Big Sam is rescuing Scarlett on the bridge from assault, and he says: "Feet, don't fail me, now". That's what I said to myself, and then the absurdity of *that* hit me like a sucker punch. Neither my feet nor my legs were failing me, and never had. I'd failed them. They were doing their damnedest to do their job. I hadn't given them what they needed - proper nutrition and exercise. Alcoholics and other addicts don't think of the long term - or the short-term consequences, for that matter. We know what was occupying our minds.

Each morning, I was wheeled to the PT room, where I began my rehabilitation . Initially, I was convinced that my PT's were all direct descendants of the guards at the Nazi work camps. In time, I realized that I might have to revise my thinking. I began to understand that they were rooting for me and celebrating with me every milestone, no matter how minuscule. At first, I made a "trip" around the outer perimeter of the PT room; a room not quite as large as a high school gym. I took three of those trips each session, interspersed with other exercises. I've tried to adequately explain to others how difficult it was, and what a triumph it became, each time I completed a round. Long before the midway point of each lap, my muscles, bones, skin - burned. It felt as though a thousand mad gremlins were jabbing me simultaneously with red-hot pokers. Ashamed, I'd steal a quick glance at "my chair", wishing I could collapse in its familiar comfort. Fat chance and thank God! That's a quick prescription for defeat. I really wasn't interested.

Another issue is footwear. Slippers are good - in fact, perhaps too good. If you think that this isn't important, guess again. One becomes accustomed very easily to navigating in soft, comfortable, light-weight slippers. When you're ready to begin the work of rebuilding your body, you'll need to invest in a pair of good, comfortable shoes. You may have been waltzing around your room, even up and down the halls, in your slippers. The first time you put shoes on, there'll be no waltzing, believe me. I got so sick of hearing "Pick up your feet, Patti. Patti, you're shuffling-again!" "No, I'm not." "Yes, you are. Listen. You can hear it." Damn! I was shuffling! Let me be very clear. I was not wearing orthopedic oxfords. I did have on a good quality, lightweight walking shoe. Honest to God, at first I thought they'd slipped ten pound weights into the soles. It's strenuous, that walking; more than you think . Never mind. You're on your way. Like it says in a book - one step at a time, one day at a time. Now, if you concentrate hard and squint a little, you can see down the road; yup, there you go! Forward, march.

Some of you may also require, as I did, a special belt that fits around your middle. It has a handle, of sorts, in the back. That's how you'll be held upright, until you can manage it on your own. When that day comes, and it will, there is hardly a greater sense of accomplishment. Eventually, your trips will take you out into the hospital/rehab complex, where you'll demonstrate your "new" skill. One thing is certain: You will NEVER take walking for granted again. Back to the PT room, and on to the other stations. They're everywhere, and you will visit each one in due course. This is as good a place as any to speak about the other "athletes" going through their paces, and the therapists at each venue. Everyone encourages everyone else. In there, no one cares who you were before, what your bank balance is or even how you ended up there in the first place. It's a great leveler. All of you have the same mission - get as much of your physical self back as you can, hopefully in better shape than when your body began to deteriorate. At first, you'll watch enviously as others do the simplest of things that you, for the moment, find impossible. Then, a therapist will quietly speak: "She's(He's) been here two weeks, and was where you are right now. You'll get there." As days pass, envy gives way to resolve, and you start believing in yourself. And, so it begins. Slowly, so slowly. Day by day. Week by week, progress. It's more astonishing when you think back to your first day. Then, out of the corner of your eye, you see her/him- a woman (or man) of indeterminate age, in a wheelchair. She looks frightened and lost. She's both. You watch as she's helped to stand, and "the belt" is placed around her. She looks over to see you watching her, and you know what you have to do. An encouraging smile and a thumbs up may do for her what they did for you, just a few short weeks ago. Then, off you go to the stationary bike where you climb on (alone!) and pedal to another place, even if it's only in your head.

One last thought on a different kind of drug therapy: Not everyone will need medication, but many will. What kind, how much, and for how long will be determined by your physician, and the physical state of your body. I was a mess. In addition to the effects of alcoholism, and subsequent withdrawal, I had also developed pneumonia. In short, I was a poster child for how not to live your life.

In order to get me back up and running, I was given a smorgasbord of pills and elixirs, each with a separate function. Unlike anti-depressants, these medications helped to heal me physically.

I can hear some of you, already. "I hate pills - I can't swallow pills- they can't make me take pills." Let's address each of those arguments separately. You hate pills? Do you hate being healthy, too? If swallowing one pill or twenty will help get you to good health, then take the pill! If you're breaking your addiction to pills in the first place, you may be given another version of the same medication - take it! It won't kill you. You went that route with the other stuff, remember? You can't swallow pills? Bull. You may not want to or like swallowing pills, but believe me, you can. If it takes a quart of water or juice to get it down, then so be it. Stop whining. Last argument: No one can make me take pills. You are absolutely right. No one can make you. A clever two-year old can figure out a way to pretend to take the pill. Actually, the two-year old doesn't even need to be clever. My point is this, while some of you may be attempting sobriety because you were forced to (legal committal), the rest of us chose sobriety. If one chooses sobriety, and yet elects to not do whatever is necessary to get well, then this question becomes necessary: Are you absolutely sure you *want* to be the best that you can be? If the answer is yes, then for heaven's sake DO WHAT YOU GOTTA DO! Some of the medication may taste like strychnine - it's not, so swallow it. There was one that I was given that not only was awful- tasting, its effect was worse. The name is Lactulose. Don't forget it. Its sole purpose is to ensure that the patient has no fewer than four – count'em 4 bowel movements per day. I haven't met the genius who decided on that magic number, but when I do (notice I said when, not if) we'll have our day of reckoning. It'll be immensely satisfying for one of us. I leave it to you to figure out which one. It was the first medication that I insisted on losing, and I must say it felt terrific taking even so small a stand. It was a symbol of my being in charge of my life. Bottom line to all of this, medication is one form of therapy used for getting you back into the game. Generally, it isn't for forever unless, as in the case of multivitamins, you want to continue taking them. Final argument: You've already done so much to improve the quality of your life. Are you willing to undo all of the good you've accomplished, because of some aversion you have to taking medication? Think about that.

You may well be thinking by now, that this is getting a little long on the therapy thing. It's your privilege, of course, to hold any opinion that you like. However, I can assure you that in all likelihood, you will be involved in some kind of therapy for the remainder of your life. Before you mentally shut down, let me explain. From this point forward, you will need to remind yourself sometimes daily, sometimes several times a day: I am not the same person I was. I respond differently than before. My responses are honest and valid. Therefore, I am valid. The reason for doing this is pretty simple. For a long time, your reaction to life was fairly one- dimensional. For women especially, it was to be pleasers. It was easy for you, (no conflict) and oddly enough comfortable in one sense, for others around you. They knew what to expect. You know what I'm talking about. This new you however, is an unknown quantity. Until such a time as the new you is as natural to you as the old one (and it will be), you must remind yourself to be strong. Those game -playing days are over. That's what I mean by being involved in therapy in perpetuity. Some of us will be lucky. The new self will take over so completely, that constant reminders won't be necessary. Others of us will need to remind ourselves frequently. It's so easy, especially in the early days of sobriety, to revert back to type. This is a good place to bring up support groups, especially AA. Some will find that they wish to incorporate an AA meeting, or a similar help group into weekly or even daily living. For those of us who choose to do so, fine. The rest of us will find other effective means of support. Lest you think that it's a sign of weakness to look outside yourself for help, remember this: Humankind is gregarious by nature. Everyone needs a connection. Like the poem says: "No man is an island." Neither, I might add, is woman. At first, daily reassurance may be necessary. In time, as you grow in strength and confidence, that need may lessen. Like I wrote earlier, bad days will be with us always. Think of them as strength-builders. Don't allow yourself to feel inferior when you find that you can't cope alone. If you need to unburden yourself, help of some kind is only a phone call away. It may be an AA partner, family member, close friend or clergy. It doesn't matter. Personally, I have attended only a couple of AA meetings since becoming sober. That's not an indictment of the program, by any means. I have a copy of the Twelve Steps, and I read them occasionally. I draw particular strength from the Serenity Prayer. My feet don't touch the floor in the morning, until I've said it. Frankly, there have been days and I'm quite sure that there are more ahead, when I give myself up to that prayer more than once a day. AA however, wasn't what I was looking for. The organization has done a tremendous amount of good, of that there's no doubt. The problem, I found, is that it is directed primarily at male drunks. Unfortunately, alcoholism isn't gender specific. There's a chapter for Wives in the Big Book, and how they should cope; there is no corresponding chapter for Husbands. Believe me, I think my husband would have benefited from one. I also have a problem with Step 6: asking for help in removing "defects of character" What? I thought that we had finally moved past that. If alcoholism is a disease, and there's no question that it is, then why is that still in the Big Book? Do diabetics, cancer patients and the like, also have defects of character that precipitated their illness? That Step is not only foolish, I think it's dangerous. It serves to perpetuate a myth; it's my opinion that it should be removed. Part of the recovery process is retrieving one's self-esteem. How anyone can expect it to happen with that thought in her head, I have no idea. I know that as a human I'm flawed. I refuse to accept that it was a character defect however, that brought on my illness.

Within the last year, I was made aware of a book, written by a woman, for other women alcoholics. In it, she adapts the 12 Steps of AA, to better suit our gender. It's good, as far as it goes. I still have a serious problem with Step 6, even with her interpretation. I discovered, quite by accident, another organization for women alcoholics, to which I'm better able to relate. It was begun by a woman, for women. The organization is called *Women For Sobriety*. Each of us has to find the appropriate key, that will help to unlock the door to a better life. What works for one, may not work for another. The important thing is to find the one that works for you.

Final thoughts on therapy: Remember how good it felt, when you finally unlocked everything that you'd hidden away for so long? You're not asking someone else to shoulder your burdens, only that he or she listens. When whatever is troubling you is out in the open, it is never quite as overwhelming as when it's allowed to hide in the dark and fester. Second, anyone who stood by you as you began your "baptism by fire" is undoubtedly still there. They didn't desert you when you were at your worst. It's unlikely that they will, as you are working towards becoming your best. So, I recommend that along with family ,friends, and therapists, you also use whatever elements of AA, or other support groups that may help, and/or the Serenity Prayer. The message is powerful: By myself, I can change no one else or no one thing. By myself, I have the power to change me, and be in charge of my response to the people and events around me. I love that feeling! I love that power! Long live Empress Patricia!

Onward and upward

Home. Now, you're ready to really start living! As I mentioned earlier, you aren't the same person; therefore it only stands to reason that your approach to life will be markedly different from what it was before BS. The biggest change, and I believe the best, will be the sense of excitement, rather than despair or dread every morning when you wake up. There will be challenges ahead; maybe you already know of one or two, say a potentially unpleasant phone call or visit. The difference is you, and your approach to that call or visit. You've got the power and you know that no matter what it is, you'll handle it. You may not like it, but you know how to cope with it. After all, what's the worst that can happen? That's easy. The worst that can happen is death. Face it, there's precious little chance of that happening. In fact, you'll find that you've dropped a common expression from your vocabulary. "I was so embarrassed, I thought I'd die!" You've been there, remember? (Like you'd ever forget!) And, while the experience was not one that you'd ever want to repeat, it didn't kill you. Actually, truth to tell, you feel more alive today than you have in a good long
time. Don't you?

I'd be less than honest, if I didn't acknowledge the fact that your emotions, for a while, will be all over the place and very close to the surface. A while back, I alluded to the problem with drug therapy; I'm not about to change horses on you now. Rather than resort to drugs to help level you out, I've got a few ideas of my own, that worked very well for me. In fact, they worked so well that I've continued them past treatment, and wouldn't give them up for anything. This is what works for me; it may help you as well. At the very least, it's worth a try.

When you chose sobriety, you made other choices also, whether or not you realize it. I know that I did. Never a breakfast eater before, I now refuse to do anything more strenuous than glance at the morning paper, until I've broken my night-long fast. That's not negotiable, and anyone who knows me, knows that. I have also chosen to continue taking a multivitamin daily. It's not prescribed, but I feel that it's necessary as part of maintaining good health. Another part of my morning routine is also non-negotiable. It's my work-out. <u>No matter what, including what time I need to be at work</u>, I take the time to do at least half of my work-out. I do the remainder of the work-out later in the day or in the evening, if necessary. Case in point: A while back, I was doing a traffic survey for the city. I had my choice of two shifts. I chose the 5:30 A.M. to 2:00 P.M. shift. On purpose, in case you're wondering. I made certain that I was up in time to eat, journal, and do half of my work-out, especially my stationary bike. It exhilarates me. Remember Towanda, Evelyn Couch's alter-ego in <u>Fried Green Tomatoes?</u> I thought Kathy Bates was extraordinary in that role. Evelyn found her power, and gave her a name: Towanda. I'll never forget what I think is her best line: "You may be younger than me and better looking, but I'm older, and have more insurance" My work-out does that for me. When I've worked up a good sweat, and my heart's really thumping, I feel like I can take on anything, and I do. Call me Kick-Ass Woman.

I also found, as I think you will too, a renewed interest in food. Notice that I didn't say good food. As far as I'm concerned, there's no such thing as "good" food. Or "bad" food for that matter, unless it's laced with arsenic. I enjoy eating, and eat what I want, when I want it. I'm healthy, energetic, and maintain an acceptable (healthy) weight. I look like what I am: a middle-aged woman. I have no interest in emulating fashion models or TV/movie celebrities. They can look the way they want. One other thing that is an inviolate part of my day, is my quiet time/journal time. It's one habit that you should at least think about cultivating. It has a calming, settling effect on me. It makes no difference when *you* do it, but I think it's important to pick one time and try to make that your time. I think you'll find that whenever you do it, it will become as important to your day as anything else that you may do. Some may choose to do it in the evening, before sleep; others, after lunch, before going back to work. My choice is first thing in the morning. I enter in my journal the people and events that impacted my life the day before. I find that allowing a day to "simmer" in my brain lets me give it the thought and perspective it deserves. When you do it isn't important. The very act of doing it will help to keep you centered. So, like the ad says: "Just do it"!

A very together woman

As long as we're on the subject of being home and doing the right thing for you, this is as good a time as any to talk about "re-creating yourself"

More than likely, through therapy, prayer or meditation, you've learned to look at yourself much differently than you ever did. That includes your physical self. If you're at all like me, you were probably not crazy about the image reflected back in the mirror. Alcohol and other drugs do a number on humans. That much is a given. What most of us don't realize when we're in the throes of the disease, is the toll it's taking on our physical appearance.

Before I go any further, I want to issue this disclaimer. I agree with those who say of our culture, that too high a premium is placed on our looks. We worship youth. You aren't going to recapture your youth. Why would you want to? But, you can undo or camouflage, for want of a better word, some of the damage . If you think that isn't important, think some more. To a certain degree, whether we like it or not, we are judged by our appearance. Most people respond to visual stimuli; I don't know of any way around that. This is what I believe: Be proud of the age you have attained, and apologize to no one. That being said however, there is no reason why anyone has to look a whole lot older than his or her chronological age, either.

What I find most astonishing, even after three years, is looking at photographs of myself from "before" and photos

of myself now. Trust me, Marie Claire will not come calling. Not today, or anytime in the future. But, the before
photos show a woman at least ten years older than my
birth certificate shows me to be. Who was that sad, old
woman? What happened? Why? Consider:

- Booze Bloat
- Skin Color - muddy
- Skin Texture - like over-worked dough
- Hair - lackluster
- Eyes - dull, lifeless
- Over-all appearance - ravaged

When I was in treatment, there wasn't a single person,
male or female who didn't fit that description.

So, what to do? For starters, you've already begun the
process. Leaching the alcohol, pills or fudge out of your
system will do wonders. Just knowing you've done that,
will lift your spirits and your self-esteem. You're eating -
healthy, this time around. You may also be engaged in an
exercise program of some kind. Those two things alone
will work miracles. The bloat will disappear. Skin color
will improve, as will over-all body tone. What else? Well,
let's see...

Body first. Undoubtedly, you've lost some weight. For
one thing, alcohol is loaded with empty calories, and calories add pounds. Take away one, you lose the other. Simple
math. The calories you're adding, in the form of food,
rather than alcohol, are the ones your body craves and will
put to good use. The amount of weight you lose, will determine your over-all body appearance - skin tone, etc.
Remember, I told you I was skinny? My skin tone left a little to be desired. Let me tell you what happened to me; it
could happen to you, too.

By the time I was released from the hospital, my skin
color had improved. I wouldn't go so far as to say I was
blooming with good health, but I no longer had the skin
color of a lemon. Besides good food and exercise, I needed
fresh air. That, my husband and I knew, was do-able. Just
get me home!

Once there, I continued my regimen of eating well, and exercising every day. My God, did I eat! Still not so much at a time, but often, like an infant. Before I began my recovery, I must have sucked the marrow right out of my bones. Actually, I tired before I filled up. My husband checked with me about every two hours, to see if I was hungry. To his utter amazement, I was every time. He'd never known me to eat so often. To my utter amazement, I'd never known me to eat so often. It was quite peculiar. We adjusted to it. It took others a bit longer. Every day, some member of my family called. The first question they asked, after inquiring about my general well-being was: "Are you eating?" They also took to asking my husband: "Is she eating? She doesn't appear to be putting on weight" Although we both understood that the questions came out of love and concern, they got old. In fact, before long we found it amusing, and considered hanging a sign around my neck: " Yes, I'm eating".

Part of the reason I think I didn't appear to be gaining, is that I was building muscle with my daily exercising. You can't see muscle, (unless you're body building) so initially I didn't look any heavier than before. But, I was. Basic truth I learned: We seldom see ourselves as others see us. Back to my skin.

One night we were lying in bed, watching T.V. I was also reading a magazine. In it was an article about people who had undergone cosmetic surgery for one reason or another. One woman had elected to have her knees done, after a considerable weight loss. She'd exercised, but for some reason was unable to tighten the skin around her knees. The surgeon removed some of the excess that had been filled with fat. I couldn't resist. I looked at my own knees. I was sitting up, with my legs stretched out in front of me. Not too bad. I've rarely been one to know when to leave things alone. I asked my husband: "Do my knees look saggy to you?" First big mistake.

He: it's kind of hard to tell when you're sitting; stand up. Caveat #1 - If you don't <u>really</u> want to know, don't ask.

Caveat #2 - If you're the "askee" honesty isn't <u>always</u> the best policy.

I stood, and raised my nightie about three inches above my knees.

He: (clearing his throat) "Well, of course, you lost a lot of weight. You've got a little skin hanging loose"

Me: (learning to know when to leave it alone) "Oh, OK" The next morning after showering, I decided to really look at myself; I have a cheval mirror in the bedroom. Taking a deep breath, I dropped the towel, and opened my eyes. One of my children's favorite books was, The Saggy, Baggy, Elephant. He and I had a lot in common. It looked as though I was wearing some one else's skin; mine certainly didn't seem to fit. My first thought was: Where did all this skin come from? I wasn't thrilled. But, I was realistic enough to know that I could improve on what was there, somewhat. I probably wouldn't get rid of all of it without surgery. You do what you think you have to or want to do. If exercise isn't cutting it after a year, and if it truly bothers you, you'll probably elect to have surgery. I chose not to have it. I've been able to tighten up and fill up a good deal of the loose skin. What's left is welcome to stick around. I'm 54, not 24. I'm fine with me just the way I am.

About the hair. I 'm one of the unfortunate few who began graying at the age of 28. For years I kept it colored, but my husband had a few thoughts of his own on the subject. His hairline had been receding slightly, (as in slightly pregnant) and he refused to consider a rug. One day, in casual conversation, he observed that if he had the grace to go bald, without wearing a toupee, I should have the grace to stop coloring my hair. I listened to him. Silly me. In spite of my hairdresser's efforts over the ensuing years, I resisted her efforts to start coloring it again. Even sillier me. Pat's a good friend as well as my hairdresser, so the topic was broached often. Still, I resisted. Silly, stubborn me. By the time I got home from the hospital, my hair had undergone even more drastic transformation. Never thick, it was now, due to poor diet and medication, thinner than before, and *really* gray.

A sister delicately brought up the subject one day. I think, fearing my response, (I'd thrown a table lamp at her once, when she asked me if I was on my knees - I wasn't.) she asked me if I had thought about maybe "doing something" with my hair.

Me: (cautiously) "Yes. Why?"
Judy: "You know, when you're ready, you should think about coloring it. I think it would give you a lift."

Me: (starting to panic) "Maybe I'm not ready yet, though." (So many changes, so little time.)

Judy: "I know. Just think about it. If you want, I'll even go with you. It'll be fun."

Me: (with relief) "Sure. Maybe later, in the spring."

Fast forward to April. Pat, my friend, my neighbor, and the best hair wizard I know, came over at my behest, carrying a large key ring with what appeared to be more than 20 scalps hanging from it. Honestly, no one could imagine a hair color not there.

Pat initially thought I should go with my original color - dark chestnut. But, I remembered hearing or reading somewhere that people should go lighter, if they decide to color at all; particularly after a "certain age". After laying several swatches on my head next to my face, we decided on "Golden Blonde". I thought it was a hoot - but decided to give it a shot anyway. Truth to tell, I had nothing to lose; my hair couldn't look any worse than it did.

The next weekend, my husband was out of town, and I decided the time was ripe. Pat performed her wizardry, and in no time, I was ready to see the results. Not only was I shocked, I was tickled right down to my socks! The color is nowhere near the color I had when I was born. It is, in my opinion, nonetheless beautiful and unless I tell otherwise, no one knows it isn't my natural color. Until reading this, of course. In fact, when one or two individuals have had the temerity to ask if it's my "natural" color, this is my standard reply: It isn't the color I was born with, but I'd like to think that *someone* on the planet was.

My point, if you haven't already got it, is: Do something nice for yourself. Maybe it's a weekly manicure or pedicure; herbal wrap, or body massage. It doesn't matter. After the knothole you dragged yourself through, you've earned it!

As for the eyes, I'll bet you've figured it out. With each passing day, as you grow healthier and stronger, the sadness disappears and the light returns. The eyes are the mirrors of the soul; for the first time, in a long time, they reflect a soul at peace. As for any errant lines or wrinkles, a few well-placed strips of scotch tape along the hair- line might help. Won't hurt.

At any rate, you feel better and look better than you have in a long time. You know it, because it's inside you. Getting older does beat the alternative. My pastor convinced me of that years ago. Anyhow, I think being 18 is highly over-rated.

Family relationships

Whenever anyone undergoes a lifestyle change, it will naturally impact not only that person, but the person's interpersonal relationships as well. The one who effects a dramatic change, whether it be a weight loss of great consequence, or getting sober, is going to seem different to those who knew that person before. There's a logical explanation: That person is different. Having made a choice to live healthy you are also, whether you realize it or not, making those subsidiary changes as well. I get annoyed when I hear complaints like: "I don't know why my friend/husband /wife, etc. thinks I've changed. I haven't. I'm the same person I always was".

Baloney. By the very fact of your sobriety, or healthy eating, you are a different person. You've taken control of your life. As a happy adjunct to that, you will find that you are no longer the passive person you were. The result may be off-putting or even threatening to the people who inhabited your life "before".

What others will find is a strong individual who knows what he/she wants, and knows what is tolerable and what isn't. In other words, you are actively engaged in living your life. The old rules you applied in interpersonal relationships won't work, because you're not the old you. Nowhere is this truer than in marital relationships. The dynamic between husband and wife, while not cast in cement, is generally believed to settle comfortably, particularly if the marriage has been one of any duration (i.e. 10 or more years).

In the past, you both knew where the buttons were and you pretty well knew what to expect when you pushed them. Not anymore. It will take time, patience and lots of understanding. It's like starting over again in your relationship. In fact, you are. As a recovering addict, you're all too aware of your own personality quirks. Through lots of hard work, you've come to recognize those things about you that need a little "fine tuning". No one is perfect; nobody expects anyone to be perfect. Your spouse will truly enjoy being around the mellower, different, sober you. However, the inevitable will happen. The subject doesn't matter. The trigger words are immaterial. At some point during the "discussion", you realize that you have very strong feelings concerning the subject under the gun, and you know that you won't back down. That puts you one step ahead of your partner. But, he'll soon catch up. Before I go any further, I need to clear something up. It's driving me batty, and I won't be able to concentrate until I've addressed the "problem". <u>All</u> of these things can and do happen to men, as well as women. But, here's the thing. I'm a woman, and this book is primarily for women, although I invite men to read it. Another thing, I think it's silly to be he/she-ing or him/her-ing all over the place. Don't you? So- if you're a male reading this, practice pronoun substitution.

Now, where was I? Oh, yes. Your partner is puzzled. Puzzled will be closely followed by temper rising, blood pressure rising and voice rising and raising. This sparring partner is brand new, and he's unprepared. What the addict has learned and put into practice, is the basic precept of the Serenity Prayer; you know what that is. I won't try to change you, or your behavior. However, I am a thinking, principled human being, and this is what my response will be. I'm not asking anyone to like it, but I will be true to myself. The strength comes from the last line:

"And the wisdom to know the difference." The battle we waged with life is over.

That is heady stuff indeed; empowerment, as it's meant to be. But, it can be very uncomfortable for other people - especially a spouse. His jury is still out on how he feels about that. It's entirely possible that he's has simply forgotten who you were, and what you were about in the first place. In time, both partners will adjust. Frankly, you'll have to, or the marriage could be in serious trouble. Remember, you didn't lose yourself or each other overnight, and it will take more than that to get yourselves and each other back. It's not easy. In fact, it would be so much easier for you to slip back into the old role each of you played. Like an old slipper, it's comfortable and familiar. Hang in there! The strength you're building will soon become comfortable and familiar also. For both of you.

My own husband, who had chosen to stick with me and help me through recovery, was alternately pleased, baffled, and irritated by the "new" wife he had acquired. He said he was proud of me, and I believed him. That, however, didn't make it any easier for him in dealing with my emotional swings, especially the first couple of weeks. He did his best to be understanding; I think had he realized that it was a natural part of the recovery process, he would have been less confused. Dare I say short-tempered, on occasion? He was also unprepared for my insecurities and, what seemed to him, unnatural fears. I had exuded, more or less, confidence in my prior approach to life whether at work or play. This timid, (yes, I was!) frightened woman was a new wrinkle for him. He knew that part of the old Patti was gone; what he didn't realize is that in order to shed that part of myself, I had been reduced to a fragile shell of a human being, and it would take time, patience, love and encouragement to help bring me into my new self. In fact, no one had told either of us what to expect. Everyone's biggest concerns were making sure that there was no booze in the house, (I have more to say about that, later) and that I had no access to guns. That one he handled beautifully on his own. He informed the psychiatrist that he never believed for a minute that I was suicidal, (bless him for his common sense!) and I had made it clear over the years, that I had no use for guns period. So, we struggled and learned, and worked things out. We're still working things out. We even, on occasion, appreciated the odd goings on inside me chemically, as well as emotionally. Not everything needs to be treated as life or death. Stop, and take a deep breath.

There's humor to be found even as you're working to rebuild your lives. Remember when you first got together? I'll bet you laughed a lot. Not at anything in particular; you just laughed because you wanted to, and it felt good. Somewhere along the line, the laughter started to die. It's not irretrievably lost, just misplaced. Find something to laugh about.

For instance: As I mentioned earlier, my hair had undergone an unpleasant change, during and after my illness.. Even after coloring it, along with " artful combing" my scalp was still visible here and there. Despite my best efforts, it was also coming out; not in clumps, but large amounts nonetheless. Also mentioned before was my husband's ongoing battle with hair loss. He'd had at one time, a headful of thick, black curls. Had. Like the lost continent of Atlantis, his hair, for the most part, is only a memory. This has never been a problem - for me. He's a little touchy on the subject. Anyway, back to my hair. Although I had gained in weight and strength, and my overall health had improved, the condition of my hair had not. A generous description would have been "will o? the wisp".

"Jeez, Patti, your hair is thin".

"Yeah, I know". What he had no way of knowing, is that I'd been to my hairdresser the day before. She'd given me very encouraging news.

My husband continued, laughing, "If you don't watch out, you'll end up as bald as I am".

Me, smiling sweetly: "Yeah, my hair's thin. That's the bad news. Good news – mine's coming back in - how about yours?"

Lest you think that this was a mean-spirited exchange, think about this: He was laughing, I was laughing, and my blood pressure remained constant, as did his; and, neither of us raised our voices. Anyway, it wasn't the first time he'd commented on my hair; it was beginning to irritate me. Besides, didn't I tell you that I was smiling sweetly? That preceding episode came along some months into my recovery. Believe me, early on, life was no drawing room comedy. I mentioned before his irritation and confusion. What I didn't see coming and wasn't prepared for, and what you may also experience, is anger. The level of anger will vary and will be prompted by different things. My husband's anger, I think, stemmed first of all by the fact that I had not "done something" before I landed in the hospital. Anger born out of financial concerns, among others. He was right, of course. To that, I have no defense. As I stated earlier, I knew before I got so sick. I think one reason for my inaction was simple fear. Fear is as great an inhibitor as it is a motivator. Without a doubt, another reason was shame. The one thing I had vowed to myself, was that I would not end up like my mother. So much for good intentions.

My husband had informed me in the fall of that year, that he was "outta here" come January 1. The drinking, although a large part of it, was not the only reason. There were other areas in our marriage that needed work. I think he hoped it would shock me into taking positive steps. It didn't. Instead of spurring me to change, it (the threat) held me in limbo, rendering me immobile. Was I in effect, attempting to end my marriage? Truthfully, I don't think so. What I was unable to see at the time, (for reasons obvious to me now) was that a fine rage had been building in me. For years, actually. Initially, I was shocked. The things that I had thought of as annoyances,

were so much more. How effectively I had them camou-
flaged! A brief explanation here might be helpful.

In 1966, my husband proposed, and I said yes. We had
talked about the future, whether or not it included children, values we held; in short, we had discussed those
matters important to any relationship. We were, for the
most part, on the same page. I thought.

Some ten years and two kids later, my spouse sprang (to
me, at least) a huge surprise. To wit, his life-long desire to
live as a cowboy. Barring that, at least as a horseman,
bringing into it all that particular lifestyle entails. Let me
make clear at the outset: I was city-born and bred. I liked
it that way. And, while I could and still do appreciate the
beauty of the equine species, I had no desire to spend even
a portion of my life perched on the back of one. I have a
healthy respect, bordering on fear, for anything that much
larger than I. You can call it cowardly. I call it prudent.
Add to that, my firm belief that even in combining our two
incomes, we lacked the financial wherewithal to sustain
such a lifestyle. Ron disagreed. Strongly. I didn't make my
case well enough, apparently. The horses arrived, followed
by a garage/barn, at great expense. That was only the
beginning. For us, an activity designed to bring a family
closer together, had the opposite effect. Of the four of us, I
was the only one who didn't ride, and had no desire to do
so. I was the one elected to office in our local saddle club.
Go figure. Add to that, every weekend spring and summer,
or so it seemed to me, was spent at horse shows. When
show season ended, the activities switched, but didn't
lessen. If my husband wasn't at work, he was at the barn.
The "hobby" had taken over our lives. To make matters
worse, my predictions of financial ruin were coming true.
Ron didn't see it. If anything, he grew ever more enamored
of the western lifestyle. I grew ever more resentful. In fairness, it's important to admit that some of the responsibility is my own. I could have made better arguments, made
a stronger stand. I didn't. I gave up trying to enlighten my
spouse's viewpoint or our lifestyle. I kept a lid on the

resentment, and numbed my true feelings with alcohol. I'd not yet learned that I had within me the power to change myself. It took years and a near tragedy before I learned the lesson. It's also important to say this: during those years there was, along with financial difficulties and my periodic resentment, some wonderful times that we shared as a couple and as a family. *Nothing* is ever all black or white, except black and white. Besides which, the feelings that had drawn the two of us together were still very strong, and we believed in and meant the vows we'd spoken to each other so many years before. Consequently, we slogged along, each of us unwilling to change; or perhaps simply not knowing how to go about it.

It's commonly accepted that hardship will do one of two things: draw a couple together, or drive them apart. As we discovered, like many other couples before us, love isn't always enough. The latter part of 1997 would force us to face up to that and deal with it, one way or another. Neither of us realized it at the time, but the clock had run out and I was already in meltdown. Two things stand out from all of this: there still exists some residual sadness that it took me so long to learn life's important lessons; secondly: if, out of a negative experience, one can emerge with new-found knowledge about herself and the world she inhabits, it's not entirely bad. I did. For that, I will be eternally grateful. And so...

As I progressed through my recovery, I happened to mention to one of my sisters that I was beginning to understand my anger, and finally learning to express it. She remarked rather dryly, that insofar as she could tell, that had never been a problem for me. (See table lamp confession). Throughout the family, including extended, my hair-trigger temper was legendary . What I hadn't understood, nor apparently had most others, is that much of my anger was misplaced. I had learned to get mad at "safe" things. Not necessarily the things that were really bothering me. Moreover, lest someone, anyone, stay mad at me, I learned to back off, and "be good" so that people would like me. I wouldn't go so far as to say today, I don't care if anyone likes me; that would be a lie. What I won't do is sell myself out, in order to avoid conflict. I consider myself a fairly intelligent person. I thought I knew the signs of suppressed anger. (Maybe I did, and didn't want to acknowledge them). I certainly thought I could recognize the signs of alcoholism. In retrospect, I know I did. I chose to ignore them. My husband's anger was justified. So was mine. This too I've learned: Unless and until both parties recognize and accept the other's anger, the healing process has no chance to begin, much less succeed.

What may create some difficulties, is the fact that you are no longer the same person you were. You may be saying to yourself – she's repeating herself. I know. Some things bear repeating; this is one of them. Your immediate family especially, has become accustomed to certain behaviors from you, for years. This new person is a stranger, and may even appear threatening in a sense. While they may have hated your old behavior, and wished you sober, and celebrated your (finally!) sober state, they don't know this person and don't recognize the behavior. The old responses, even negative ones, are familiar and in their own way, reassuring.

Another case in point: One afternoon, my husband and I were engaged in a heated discussion; he was angry about something that had nothing to do with what I was wearing, yet he knew what to say, to raise my insecurity and in doing so, weaken my resolve. He found the button that in the past had been powerful enough to immobilize me. "Why do you wear those pants? They make your ass look twice as big as it is". The wrong thing to say, at any time. The "old Patti", ever sensitive to her figure would have been demoralized to the point of dropping the argument, leaving the room, and ultimately changing the pants for others. He forgot that I'd left her at the bottom of the bottle, where she belonged. I turned on him, and spat back that I would wear whatever I damned well pleased, my ass was just fine, and if he didn't like it, he could .. . Well, let's just say it would have been physically impossible, and leave it at that. He was stunned. I was too. I was also euphoric. He had known, of course that one thing had nothing at all to do with the other, but it was a ploy that had worked before. Old methods of dealing with one another won't work. When I had cooled off we talked, and I think for the first time he understood that his old responses were going to elicit brand new responses from me. Call it whatever you want: equalization, shift in the power balance, it really makes no difference. As a recovering addict, I was merely learning what the rest of the world had known for a long time. I have (you do, too)my own personal power, and the right to exercise it. While you may be fine with that, (I was and am), others may need a bit more time. Actually, what everyone needs is time. You're all navigating unfamiliar waters. Sometimes the ride is breathtakingly beautiful; sometimes it's scary as hell. Hang in there. All of you. Life will get better. I didn't say easier; just better. It already has, you know. You're not drinking, are you?

So, as Ron and I moved through my recovery, we learned all over again, how to appreciate each other, and show it. My renewed interest in life led to a renewed interest in my spouse. Not earth shattering news, exactly. But, when a couple has been drifting in opposite directions for a protracted period of time, in order to regain a relationship, it's important to take an interest in what the other is doing and thinking. And doing things with each other, that perhaps you've forgotten how to do over the years. We talked. Often. The subject wasn't always earth-shattering; we'd had a belly-full of earth shattering, anyway. One thing that stands out, was that even in the midst of his sometime anger, my husband found the time and unique ways to demonstrate that he cared. For example, when I first arrived home, I was able to walk without a walker or any other contrivance, but some things were still beyond me. I could sit down by myself; getting up was a trick, unless I had something to use as a brace. The bathroom proved to be a challenge. My thoughtful, resourceful husband used oak railings that he had stashed in the garage, and built a kind of "chair to fit over the toilet, so that I could use it to "lift off". A "throne for the throne", you might say. He also added a hand railing for me to use for going into our family room, two steps down. It afforded me much needed, and thus appreciated, independence. We *both* appreciated that.Before I leave this section, I think it's important to explain a comment made earlier, concerning my mother. She lived a large part of her life as an alcoholic. She died as one. Far too young, (age 56) as far as all of us who knew her were concerned. Had she been able to exorcise the demons that plagued her, I believe we would still be enjoying the company of that very bright, often charming, and interesting woman. Sadly, for her family and friends, not to mention for herself, she was unable to do so. As I began my own private descent into hell, my thoughts were often drawn to her. And then, just as quickly dismissed. I didn't want it to be true, and so tried to block the reality from my mind. A funny birthday card was circulating some years back: "Another year older, another year closer to looking like Mom". One year, TWO of my sisters gave me that card! If they only knew! With them, I laughed. Alone with my thoughts, my blood ran cold. I was already circling the drain, only they didn't know it and I wasn't ready to admit it. Just like Mom. Lucky for me, someone made one last try. That time, the message got through. Next stop: The Recovery Resort, courtesy of Altru Hospital.

Children

As recovering alcoholics, most of us know about the 12 Steps associated with AA. Step 4 deals with acknowledging the harm you did, and apologizing and making amends, where possible.

For the recovering female alcoholic, the last part of Step 4 may be difficult. In fact, in one sense, it is impossible. We are, many of us, mothers. And, while there's no question that we can and should acknowledge and apologize to our children for the harm we did them, I don't see how it's possible to make amends. Let's be honest here. Can you turn back the clock and give them back all or a portion of their childhood? The answer begs the question. We can't go back. No one can, for any reason. So then, the real question becomes how to carry out the last part of Step 4. Most children, adult or not, will be thrilled by your sobriety. It is something that they've hoped for and perhaps prayed for, for a long time. Their euphoria may last days, weeks or even months. Eventually however, they're going to crash, at least to one degree or another. It's common, and personally, I think they're entitled. They rode an emotional roller coaster all of their own, but beside you and with you nonetheless, as you struggled first in denial and then in the initial stages of recovery. There is a way, should your children be willing to accept it. At some point they will level out, and realize what is obvious to everyone but them : All parents are human beings. All human beings are flawed. Therefore all parents are flawed. They have made mistakes. They will continue to make mistakes. No rational parent, recovering addict or not, can honestly deny causing their children pain of one sort or another. However, I also believe that no rational parent ever set out to deliberately ruin a child's life. Poor choices result in lousy outcomes. That is to me an immutable fact. So, the question remains: How to make amends? The way, I think, is in showing them that you are living a healthy life; healthy for yourself and all those around you. Don't think for a minute that I'm dismissing out of hand the feelings that children will have. I'm not telling them to "Get over it". I am the child of an alcoholic. I know too well what children are thinking and feeling. Nevertheless, to dwell forever in the past, reliving old hurts produces nothing positive. I see it as tantamount to picking at a scab. The wound may eventually heal, but it will take much longer than if it's acknowledged, and then allowed to heal. Part of the process is forgiveness. Children will have to find their own way to forgive, and in their own time. It may not fit our timetable, but there it is. It would be, I believe, too much to expect them to forget. I think that would be asking them to deny their past. Unlike some, I don't happen to believe that forgiving and forgetting necessarily go hand in hand. It is possible to have the one without the other. That said, if they are to forgive you, you must also forgive yourself. You may find, as I did, that to be the most challenging task ahead of you. It is also the most important. How can you possibly move forward if you're still looking back? Besides, you don't want to turn into a pillar of salt, do you? I really don't mean to make light of so serious a topic. Self-forgiveness is another issue. I'll address it in a later chapter.

It would be foolish to suggest that any child/parent relationship is one continual barrel of laughs. If any prospective parent thinks so, they amend those thoughts within the first week that the new child is home. So too, will relationships alter between the alcoholic parent and her children. As I said before, no one can go back. There will be the issue of trust. Children may not trust your sobriety right away. That's OK. You know, and by the simple act of watching you live your life sober, your children will come to realize that they can trust again. When that happens, good times are not only possible, they can almost be guaranteed. In fact, one of my most cherished memories with my son, occurred about six months into my sobriety. Here's what happened.

My son is a music maven. No, that won't do. He doesn't simply eat, sleep and breathe music, he absorbs it through his pores. <u>Any and all music.</u> I like some music; some kinds much more than others. I happen to be a "boomer". Class of 1964, to be exact. Do you remember where you were and what you were doing on Feb. 4, 1964? I can tell you precisely where I was, and what I was doing in exquisite detail. Stumped? Think Ed Sullivan. Think Brit. Think the Beatles, for goodness sake! Like every other teenage girl back then, I was swept along on a tidal wave of Beatlemania. I loved them and their music. I still do. A Christmas gift from one of my best friends that Dec., 1963, was their first album, "Meet the Beatles". My son coveted that album. The first time I played it for him, he was transfixed. After that, I often found him on a rainy day, flipping through our collection of albums, only to grab "MTB", and study it quietly. Age 6, age 10, and age 20 - <u>that</u> about him never changed. Also, never so crass as to ask "When you're dead, can I have this?", he nonetheless would ask: "Someday, can I have this?" I'd merely smile, and say "someday".

His 26th birthday rolled around shortly after my release from the hospital. There is nothing particularly remarkable about a 26th birthday, except that it is another year to celebrate life. But, it was on this pedestrian birthday, that I chose to gift him with "The Album". It was, of course one way for me to thank him for all of the love and support he'd shown me. More importantly, I wanted him to understand that a new day had dawned, and that "someday" has real meaning. To a child, "someday" can be as elusive as a butterfly. What better way to tell him that "someday" has substance and "someday" is now? Although none of those thoughts was articulated by either of us that day, (except, naturally, my thank you) I believe he understood my motivation. He has it proudly displayed in his living room.

Up to this point, I've avoided mentioning my oldest child. Perhaps avoided might be disingenuous. I wasn't ready to speak of the person or the relationship. Period. I'm still not at all certain that I can begin to do justice to the saga, for that is exactly what it is. I'll try. On December 21, 1968, a nurse informed me that I had a "beautiful baby girl". Today, nearly 33 years later, that same child sports a goatee. I believe an explanation might be in order .

Mother/daughter relationships can be described as "tricky" at times. This might be an understatement in describing my relationship with my daughter - or, lack of it. We have, over the years, shared both laughter and tears as do, I suspect, most mothers and daughters. We have shared much in common, she and I. We love books - all books, Gone With the Wind - all manifestations, women's issues, and Ritz Crackers; not necessarily in that order. She is: bright, warm, articulate, witty, and at times I think, too smart for her own good. Those are all a part of her charm. She is also stubborn, willful and unyielding. Those, too, are a part of her charm. She is a very strong person. I'm glad. I'd like to think that I can take some of the credit for that. As she should, she holds me accountable for my behavior, and the impact it had on her. I also get the sense, however, that she holds me responsible for most of the hurt that she has experienced. That is one area where we differ. This much I know now: She struggled, more and longer with her gender than I ever knew. Oh, that I had been more intuitive! I know, of course, about children being born one sex physically, but having the emotional wiring of the opposite. That it had happened to

one of my own, never crossed my mind. Would I have done
better or differently had I known? I cannot, in all honesty
say. Perhaps, as the years passed, and she grew into a
young woman, had I not drunk I might have noticed her
anger. In truth , I did. I attributed it, in a large sense, to
teen-age angst. As for anything else, I simply didn't know.
Certainly, there were plenty of times where my judgement
was clouded by nothing more than day to day concerns;
doing the same things as other mothers. Non-drinking
mothers. As I think back, in my mind's eye, I see a woman
busy juggling a teaching career and family, making
choices and acting on them. Not always wisely, it turned
out, but never with malicious intent. In any case, a frustrated young woman grew up under my roof, while I
remained clueless. Teenage girls tend to be mercurial, as I
knew from my job. Maybe that's why I missed it. I don't
know. I do know this: In between the outbursts (hers, followed by mine) and the tantrums (again, both of ours)
there was also shared laughter, communion, and joy.
Photographs don't always lie. Anyway. She attended the
local state university for one year, and then chose to leave
for Minneapolis and the University of Minnesota. More
opportunity, she said. Grand Forks was too stifling. We
had no idea. As time passed, she came home occasionally
on weekends, and nearly always for holidays. About two
years after her move to the cities, she came home one
week-end with her hair cut. I mean *cut*. She'd told us
about it beforehand, but nothing could have prepared us
for the reality. Absolutely nothing. In the next year, we
had occasion to spend time with her in Minneapolis. After
that, I had a growing sense that there was more to her life
than she was allowing us to see. She was well over 18; it
really wasn't for us to say how she should be conducting
her life. The next summer, she came out to her dad and
me; she had come out to her brother some time before.
Frankly, I wasn't that surprised, nor was my spouse, as we
had discussed the "what ifs" once or twice before. In all
honesty, neither of us can say that we were happy about

the fact that our daughter is a lesbian. Nevertheless, she seemed to us to be at peace with herself, mostly relieved at our response, and genuinely happy. We're no different than most parents, in that what we wanted most for both of our children was their safety, and well-being. We know what's out there, and like parents everywhere, we worried all the time about her in the big city. We knew that this wouldn't make it any easier. As I said, our children's happiness was paramount, so long as that happiness didn't come at the expense of another human being. This certainly wasn't the case. Lastly, neither my husband nor I subscribe to the idea that gays and lesbians choose their lifestyle any more than a heterosexual chooses. We believe that we are what we were born to be.

In 1995, she broke off contact with all members of her family. She had, in the past, tried to communicate her frustration with me, her father and our drinking habits. She gave it up as a lost cause. In retrospect, I understand now that she had no other choice. I also know that her efforts were no less than her sibling's were some few years later. Still, her observations and requests went unheeded. Why? I'm not positive, but: The answer, I think, lies in the willingness to hear the message. In reality, it has not so much to do with the messenger, or the method of delivery, as it does with the timing of that message. The recipient must be ready to hear the words. If that person isn't ready, the words spoken take on an entirely different meaning. The real message gets lost; the interpretation is not at all what the messenger had in mind. This, of course, leads to the question: What makes anyone "ready?" This is almost impossible to answer. It is especially, if the message is perceived as unpleasant or uncomfortable. That is the way, I think, of most human beings. Few of us willingly listen to a message that may be construed as critical. That's protection of self, at the most basic level. If anyone reading this has the solution to solving this dilemma, let me know. I'd be forever grateful. So, I think, would millions of others. What finally allows a bigot to see what a non-bigot sees? What forces have been at work, permitting more religious tolerance, at least in some parts of the world? I don't know. I do know this: There is still much to be done as regards tolerance, whether with respect to religion, gays, lesbians, race or ethnicity. But, back to my main point: A. tried. I will not say she failed. I believe, with every fiber of my soul, every addict knows. Acknowledgment is something completely apart. Do I wish my antennae (and I) had been more receptive? Naturally. It would have saved all of us, especially A., from so much pain. That I couldn't /wouldn't/didn't "hear", is a regret that will be with me always. Will I dwell on it? No. As much as I love to write, I can't re-write history. I can hope that in time, with patience, A. will understand, and find his/her own way to forgive me. That's all anyone can ask of another human being.

In the interest of her own mental health and well being/preservation, she removed herself from our lives. She remained "hidden" from all of us until recently. We had made some attempts at contact; far too few. At various times, we called her last known number; it had been disconnected. I also sent a couple of letters; to the wrong address, as it turned out. I know now the steps we could have taken and didn't. There's a German/Pennsylvania Dutch expression that I think might best explain much of what we say or do, (or don't) and later regret: "We get too soon old and too late smart". The saddest part in all of this is the enormous price we paid. All of us.

Thankfully, in August of 2000, she broke her silence and wrote to our son. She has taken more definitive steps to alter her body both physically and emotionally, hence the goatee. She has told our son that she isn't ready for us yet. Honestly, neither one of us is ready for her yet, either. I look at pictures that we have, and my brain simply refuses to make the leap. I know that there are other transgenders out there and acceptance of them is relatively easy for me. It's quite another thing, when it is your own child. My son tells me that she is less agitated and angry and more at peace than he's ever known her to be. For that, I'm grateful. I can't and won't speak for my husband, but this is exactly how I feel: She/he is my child, always will be. Nothing she/he does or I do will change that. I love her/him. Nothing will ever change that. From this point forward, I have to make some changes in how I think of this person, my eldest child. He, not she. Him, not her. So many changes and surprises. For her, too, I think. After reading this last part, you may be wondering, "Where's the humor in this?" To tell you the truth, I don't think there is a whole lot. There is this, however. There's humor, and there is "to be in good humor". While I've not yet found occasion for a huge laugh about this rather strange turn of events, I must confess to feeling slightly amused by the thought of A. in facial hair. If this seems to you to be too frivolous an attitude, I simply refer you to Oscar Wilde: "Life is too important to be taken seriously". Believe it or not, I am in good humor, concerning my first born. A. is safe; of primary importance to me, as her child's safety would be to any mother. A. is finding peace. I know how important that is. As for the rest, I will wait and see. "After all, tomorrow is another day".

You may wonder why I've chosen to share this particular information about my daughter with you. First of all, once you become a mother, you are always a mother; that said, anything that impacts your child's life, will impact your own in one way or another. In this instance, while I applaud my child's courage and am grateful for the new - found peace in her/his life, I fully understand that my daughter, as I knew her, has ceased to exist. In that one sense, it is not unlike losing a child to death. For any mother, parent really, there can be no greater loss, than that of a child. The argument can be made of course, that my child is very much alive, and he is; she, with all the permutations of her former gender, is not. Therein lies the difficulty, from my point of view. My final point is this: no matter what the change or upheaval, and this qualifies as the latter, at least in my mind, if you have peace within, you will eventually come to be at peace with whatever may come your way. Without the "help" of alcohol, or any other drug.

Except for that one brief anecdote earlier, I haven't told you much about my son. It is he, you understand, who firmly but gently, with love and courage, confronted me and my drinking. He was able to accomplish, that which A., despite several efforts, had not. Why? As I said before, I don't have the answer to that question. Deep down, I knew. I honestly believe that all addicts know. In the light of day, surrounded by everyday activity, denial comes easy. But, in the dark of night, alone with only your thoughts, denial evaporates and reality finally creeps in. I can only imagine the pain he endured when he decided to speak up. By his very nature, he is non-confrontational. How desperate and frightened he must have been! With the strength and courage of a thousand super-heroes, he spoke the words that finally registered and forced me to take stock; and in so doing, take back my life. Every day, in my heart, I thank him. Every day, I thank him by living sober. I can think of no better way to show my gratitude.

This is not to say that he hasn't produced challenges in my journey. Some eight months into my sobriety, his marriage dissolved. It was painful and messy for everyone. No marriage disintegrates on its own. There is blame and credit enough for all. My husband and I ached for our son, daughter-in-law and most especially for our two grandchildren. Though without question the most innocent, they paid the highest price. That is the real tragedy in any divorce where there are children. Throughout it all, we were powerless to do much of anything, but stand by and watch. It's awful, and I wouldn't wish it on anyone. It never occurred to us to not support our son. That's not to say that we always agree or approve of everything he does. Love the person, I say. You may never understand or like the behavior. It is possible to divorce the two. That, to me, is the essence of family. He has been and continues to be a remarkable young man. He has been called on to walk a path not of his choosing, that of liaison between us and our oldest child. He does so with gentleness and grace. I'm not surprised, for that is the essence of him. As I ponder all this, the irony is inescapable. I gave him life; in return, he helped give mine back to me. As he was and continues to be for me, I will be for him.

More family

Family is family is family. Also true: You can pick your friends, but you can't pick your relatives. In my case, as I hope it is in yours, my family, whether by blood or through marriage, gifted to me the one thing that above all else that can help to ensure success in recovery. Love - no strings attached, non-judgmental, compassionate, understanding love. When you are in the first stage of recovery, there's little or no self-love; not even the healthy kind. Love is what will help you get to stage two, reclaiming your self-esteem. You can't live your life without it; you know where it is. My family saw what I couldn't: a worthwhile, lovable human being. It was they who helped me find the courage to head down a very frightening path, when my compass seemed to be spinning in a state of confusion. That's not to say that I didn't recognize the benefits of sobriety. I did - physically. But, after my meltdown, I felt like pieces of me were scattered all over. I wanted to pick them up and put me back together again, I just didn't know how all the pieces fit. I knew how they fit before. Now, I wasn't so sure. I had some sleuthing to do. Who is that woman in the mirror? The calling and cards, calling and flowers, calling and visiting, helped me to stay on course, pick up the pieces, and reconstruct the person that had been lurking there all along. Discovering my reality in this way was illuminating. And it beat the hell out of pinching myself. There were, however, some awkward moments.

Scarcely a week after my hospital release, my husband, I think in an effort to reassure himself that I was "fine" and we were back to "normal" decided we should have his sister and her husband for dinner. "It will be fun", he said. "We need to say "thank you" in a special way", he said. "I'll do all the work", he said. Two out of three ain't bad.

I agreed that we did indeed owe them. We owed so many. Oney and Len had been there for him, in every way, while I was incapacitated. They fed him, sat with him, supported him, and even loaned him a car when his pick-up died.

He did do all the work. Steak on the Jenn-aire, salad from a bag, and hash browns; the work was all his. As for fun. In retrospect, it was; a little. Mostly, I was terrified. They had seen me when I wasn't exactly at my best; I hadn't seen them much. I'd spoken to them, of course. Actual seeing, that was something else. Ron placed the call. They accepted. He got things ready. I got nervous. The appointed hour approached, arrived and then passed. Where were they? They lived across town, not across the state, for heaven's sake. Finally, the doorbell rang, and we both went to answer it. I had done the best I could to make myself presentable. Even I knew that we're only allotted so many miracles in a lifetime. I already had mine: My family and friends were coming to visit me in my home, not the cemetery, Anyway. We knew each other well. In spite of that, (!) we'd always enjoyed each other's company. That was a plus. Though the time for pretense had long since passed, Len's comment threw me.

They: "Sorry we're so late."

Us: "We were afraid you couldn't make it - like something came up."

Len: "It did. I was afraid to see you. The last time I saw you really scared me".

He was afraid to see me. How little we know the ones we think we "know" so well. We had a great evening.

Wonderful conversation, tasty food, and lots of laughs. This same scene was to repeat itself many times over the next several months. Though others may not have understood my trip to the "netherworld" or my justifications for taking it in the first place, they nevertheless demonstrated kindness and compassion. Every word, every gesture, helped me. In a very short time, I learned to relax and enjoy myself in their company. One step closer to becoming a whole person.

During the evening mentioned above, we also had wine - non-alcoholic. Before you go ballistic, remember, not everyone is alike - not even alcoholics. I had determined after much thought (5 weeks in the hospital will do that) that there wasn't a chance under the sun that I would surrender the crystal wine goblets I had waited for, for so long. What's wrong with juice or soda? What's wrong with milk? Nothing. I like the look of wine in a wine goblet, pure and simple. For me, as it is for many alcoholics, it's not about the taste of the wine that will drag you down that path again. As I pointed out to one of my sisters, if alcoholism were about taste, there'd be no market for Ripple or Thunderbird. Most alcoholics are going for the effect. I was one of those. I recognize that there are some for whom the taste will trigger the desire for the real thing. For many of us, that is not the case. O'Doul's does a brisk business, as do many vintners that produce a non-alcoholic version of their most popular varieties. To my fellow addicts: You alone will know if those beverages are for you. You know better than anyone why you chose alcohol as a coping mechanism. I mentioned before, how adamant the psychiatrists were in making certain that no alcohol be anywhere near me for a long time, if ever. Let me close this diatribe (I still have a few anger management issues) with this one thought: Anyone who desires a drink of alcohol will find a way to get it. It's simply naive to think that by removing it from the immediate reach of the addict, she'll be out of harm's way. Necessity is the mother of invention. If an alcoholic thinks she needs a drink, she'll find one - or six. Make no mistake about it. Lesson learned that night: Don't assume anything about anyone, including yourself. Remember: Uncharted waters.

Friends

The best way, I think, to reconnect with friends is in the comfort and security of your home. I recommend that you do it slowly, one friend at a time. Also, be prepared to undergo some scrutiny. People are naturally curious; and, you've been out of circulation for awhile. While they know that you've undergone change, they'll look for manifestations of that change. Let them look. You'll also discover who your real friends are. Most people today recognize addiction for what it is - a disease. Thank God the days of stigma and social shunning are becoming a thing of the past. But, there are some who, for reasons of their own, may choose to not be a part of your life any longer. Should that happen, realize that it may have happened anyway. Friends drift apart all the time, for many reasons. They form new alliances all the time. So can you.

One of my friends, who was there before, during and in fact still is, wanted to come see me after I got home from the hospital. She called, and we set a date and time. Again, I was nervous. I was taking myself up one level in human engagement, and although I trusted Lois implicitly, I harbored a good deal of insecurity. In the hospital is one thing; out changes everything. There's safety in being a patient, which I no longer was. Coincidentally, I'd been through hell, and looked it. My husband has a quaint expression he uses once in awhile. It fit. I definitely looked like I'd been "rode hard and put away wet". In other words, not quite ready for the cover of Vogue.

On the other hand, unlike the last visit she made, this time I was dressed, not confined to a bed, and navigating on my own (more or less). I figured those had to be pluses.

When she arrived that afternoon, we chitchatted about this and that; superficial perhaps, but safe. I know she sensed my nervousness, but graciously chose not to comment on it. After a few moments, we had settled into the easy conversation we had previously enjoyed. It was then that she handed me a package. Inside was a small, rectangular mirror. Wrapped in tissue next to it was a porcelain rose.

She said to me: "Lay the mirror on a flat surface, and place the rose atop it. The mirror reflects back the beauty of the rose. "But more than that", she continued, "once in a while, remove the rose and the reflection you see will be one of beauty, also".

Lois saw what I was unable to see. Not heart-stopping, breath-taking beauty, but the best kind of beauty of all. That which comes from within, when the soul is finally at peace. Like true friends do, Lois gave me the greatest gift she could have: Courage to look at myself, and believe in the possibilities. I was in my larval stage. Could there be a butterfly in there somewhere?

One other illustration comes to mind concerning colleagues and generosity. Although it took place nearly three years ago, I'm still humbled by the memory. Through one brief exchange, I believe I stumbled onto an act of grace. The dictionary gives us this definition: "Grace: Beauty of form, movement or manner; pleasing or agreeable quality or feature; God's free and undeserved favor to and love for mankind; influence of God operating in man to improve and strengthen".

Of all the support, perhaps the most gratifying yet terrifying was that extended to me from colleagues and friends at the high school where I had taught for ten years. Gratifying, because in spite of what had happened with me, they demonstrated repeatedly that they were "with me". It terrified me because of the shame I felt, and understanding that I'd have to come face to face with them one day. Telephone calls are one thing; physical confrontation is another. The fear I felt in knowing that I *had* to visit them in no way abrogated the fact that I *wanted* to visit. I thought of it as a kind of "bearding the lion". A few months after my release, on a beautiful May day, I realized that I was ready to visit my colleagues at the high school where I'd previously taught. There was no single event to tell me I was ready; I just knew. Paradoxically, I was riding a physical and mental high, while at the same time I was scared witless. Liken it to your first airplane ride: great anticipation, coupled with a fear of the unknown.

I parked the car and began what seemed like the longest hike of my life. I made for the head office, having earlier determined that it would be my first stop. I spied John, an associate principal, just inside the door. John and I had enjoyed a pretty good relationship in the past. Weak-kneed, I approached him; I was determined to keep about me some semblance of dignity, while conveying everything I felt in my heart. My determination not withstanding, my voice broke as I reached to shake his hand and whisper a heartfelt "thank you". With a gentle smile, John grasped my hand and said, "For what?"

To this day, it's difficult to explain precisely what those words meant to me. In that two-word question lies the embodiment, I believe, of that which is true grace. Each of us, at one time or another, has been buoyed by triumph, only then to be hobbled by adversity. It's my hope that when adversity strikes, each will be as I was that day, also cushioned by grace.

Since that encounter, I have tried to live my life sharing grace as I have come to understand it . John's gift, like that of so many others, helped to bring about a change in my outlook. Where there was once despair and cynicism, there is now hope. In a soul that knew mostly conflict, there now resides mostly peace. This is due, I think in no small measure to the grace of God through John, and two little words, "For what?"

While those two occasions spring to mind immediately, they were by no means the only instances of my friends' support. Whether from the neighborhood or through work, or friends who coincidentally were also family, they gathered around me protectively yet without smothering me, gifting to me the time to learn how I fit in this new world of mine.

There are times when I think I never saw things as clearly as I do today. I know now, I didn't understand life completely or the role I have been assigned to play in it. As it must be with many others, the frustration in my life was in large part of my own making. Wishing something is so will not make it so. This is true, I think, of any relationship. The lesson learned, painstakingly and painfully, came to me rather late in life. Better that I had learned it earlier? Probably. The fact remains that I didn't; as a result, I learned lessons within lessons. In retrospect, I think that this is not all bad.

Because of changes brought about by choices I have made in the last few years, I see the world and consequently the people in it, through different eyes. I'm not *quite* so quick to judge; who am I after all, but another human being making her way as best as she can. Not a saint; that much is clear. I stumble, and occasionally end up sprawled flat on my face. That is the way with all people. The difference in myself, as far as I can tell, is that I'm determined to get back up and try a different approach. It may also be my willingness to recognize that once in a while, I'm my own biggest obstacle.

A sister once commented that she has seen a "softer" side to me, that hadn't been readily apparent before. I don't know about that. Perhaps it is no more than the absence of pent-up anger, and the relief I've experienced from the release of that.

This much I do know: All of my friends played an invaluable supportive role, as I made my way out of my cocoon, and back into the world a different, hopefully better, definitely stronger person than I was before. No one can ask any more of friends than that.

Entertaining

Earlier, I touched briefly on the subject of entertaining at home. I think it merits more attention. If you are at all like me, you liked to entertain before - at least usually. As you get stronger physically and mentally, you're going to find yourself wanting to get back into the fray socially; and *really* enjoy yourself. I found it best, (read easiest) for me if I kept it small and at home, rather than in a restaurant. (Restaurants require careful navigation. More about that, later.) Obviously, the people you choose as guests will be those with whom you feel most comfortable. That is to say, right now might not be the perfect time to entertain your spouse's new boss. That can be a hair-raising experience under the best of circumstances. This isn't it. So hold off. But, you can entertain with elan, as soon as you're physically ready. Don't wait until you think you're ready mentally. Chances are, you'd put it off until most of the guest list was either in a rest home, or a more permanent "resting place". You're stronger than you think. The first few times you entertain will be a little nerve wracking, no matter who it is or when you do it. So, here's what you do:

10 STEPS TO SUCCESSFUL ENTERTAINING
1. Give yourself a pep talk. You had a *drinking* problem, not a *cooking* problem. It didn't obliterate your culinary skills. (Remember, we went over that.)
2. Use the phone - invite someone over.

3. Say the Serenity Prayer.

4. Get crackin'

5-9. Keep moving - Optional: Say the Serenity Prayer as many times as you like - out loud, if you want to. Put it to music, if necessary.

10. ENJOY YOURSELF! You've earned it.

A word about food preparation: If, like me, you enjoy cooking and particularly like cooking ethnic, many of your recipes are going to call for liquor of some kind. Relax. First of all, most recipes that call for wine won't suffer in the least if you use water or broth. One exception: Boeuf Bourguignonne. Beef Burgundy, for pity's sake! You can do a couple of different things. 1. Drop the recipe from your repertoire. Recipes are like fish in the sea - there are millions of'em out there. 2. Adapt the recipe. Use cooking wine; simply eliminate salt from the remainder of the recipe; cooking wine is loaded with salt. One point to remember is that the wine gives flavor; the alcohol is cooked out. Some of you may be thinking: Well, even if it's cooking wine, it's still wine. You're right. Consider this: Read the alcohol content by volume on a bottle of vanilla. Go ahead – I'll wait. You're back? Good. Answer me this. Are you ready to give up chocolate chip cookies? Any cookies? Cake? I thought not. Me either. If, for any reason, this doesn't work for you, see # 1. Whatever you do, don't whine about some dish being your specialty. Get a new one.

Just a couple of other random thoughts. You need to decide if you're going to provide your guests with an alcoholic cocktail before dinner, or "real" wine with the meal. If you choose not to, don't give it another thought. You're one of a growing number of hosts who has decided to eliminate that from the festivities. No one will object. If someone does...hmmm, you gotta wonder why, don't you?

On the other hand, let's be realistic. You've made your choice. Not your spouse's; not your guests'. They are capable of making their own decisions. However, you can and should set limits. After all, it's your house, and your party.

Many of the experts caution against being around alcohol at all, and certainly not in the first few months of sobriety. One word - Get a grip! OK, that's three. You can't expect the world to change, because you have (had) a problem. Let others indulge, if they want to. That doesn't mean that you shouldn't step in if someone you know and care about is going over the limit - or is gone. But, that's it. You can't shoulder someone else's consequences. No one can. "God, grant me the serenity..."

Depending on how you look at it, social acceptance of alcohol can be a good thing or a bad one. The real point is: This time, it's not going away. It's been proven, prohibition doesn't work. Unless you want to live like a hermit, (and most people don't) you'll have to adjust. I doubt that this is the first adjustment you've had to make. Remember? You just did it, and got on with your life. If it is the first time, it's about time. Who do you think you are, anyway? Seriously, you're going to find that the business of living is most enjoyable without artificial stimulants. Do you recall childhood birthday parties? Was alcohol served? Did you have a good time?

The longer I'm alive, the more convinced I've become, that adults should "take a page out of children's books" in learning how to live, instead of the other way around. If you think that's an odd idea, consider this: Children *find* joy in nearly anything; most grown-ups spend their adult lives *seeking* it. There's an important lesson there. And I don't think that's backward thinking, even if I am left-handed. So there.

Restaurants & Bars

Yes, you read correctly. Bars. Many eating establishments have a bar area, that at the very least, you may have to walk through. At the worst, you may be asked if you want to "wait in the lounge and we'll call you when your table is ready". So. You need a game plan, unless you already have one. Running and screaming in the other direction isn't an option. Neither, of course, is having alcohol. But you can go in, order a "cold one", drink it, enjoy it, and feel good about your choices. You know what they are . Bartenders are in the service industry; think of something you like and ask for it. It's that simple. They may not have exactly what you want, so be prepared with a second choice.

Example: I discovered that I like "Virgin Mary's"- prepared my way, with V-8, not plain tomato juice. I'll take them with tomato juice, but I mention, ever so nicely, that they really are better with V-8, so maybe she/he should mention it to the barkeep, who in turn might mention it to the person who does the ordering for the bar in the first place. Often, they'll get the message right quick. See, they know too, there are lots of watering holes out there. They need you; you hold the purse strings. Simple economics. Also, don't be embarrassed or God forbid too intimidated to ask for something like a non-alcoholic margarita or daiquiri. Don't be put off by the fact that you'll probably have to go to the children's menu. Listen up, restaurant owners. Not everyone who wants a non-alcoholic beverage is under 21. We only look like it. Kidding. I'm not kidding, however, in my request. It's simply a matter of putting some thought into placement of items in the menu. While we're still in the bar - and aren't you having fun being there and being sober? - a word to the wise bar/restaurant owner. Make certain that your wait staff is savvy enough to serve a grown up a beverage in a grown up glass. Not plastic. Case in point: Not too long after I was released, my husband and I decided to go to a local Mexican restaurant for dinner. We both ordered what we wanted, including a beverage. I ordered a non-alcoholic Margarita, my husband a Corona beer. He got a frosted glass mug for his drink, I got a plastic water tumbler for mine. Other customers, having "real" Margaritas, were sipping theirs from a Margarita glass. First off, I hate drinking from plastic. Second of all, I had ordered a grown-up drink, even though it was on the child's page. I felt insulted. All around me, other adults were being treated as adults. Because I had chosen from the "child's page", I was being treated like a child. Heads up, wait persons of the world: Pay attention to who is ordering what.

I didn't say anything until we got in the car, and then I exploded. Fat lot of good that did. But - I vowed that the next time, and there was no doubt that there would be, I'd make darn sure I got a grown-up glass.

It so happened that we were in another city, at a Mexican restaurant of the same chain, shortly after that. I politely requested that my peach/mango non-alcoholic Margarita be served in a regular Margarita glass. My wait person equally politely informed me that *all* Margaritas were served in the appropriate glass. I was pleased; so was she... she got a great tip! We've had occasion to go back to the same restaurant in our hometown - the food is excellent and so is the atmosphere. However, I have to request each time that my drink be served appropriately. I don't know why I should have to. It may seem like a small thing, but it's important to me. Actually, it should be important to everyone. It's about dignity.

The first time out to a restaurant can be intimidating. It doesn't have to be. Face up to the fact that you may run into people you knew before. So what? They may be curious; they may not. Again, so what? You're probably thinking that it's easy for me to say now, from the vantage points of time and distance, that it's no big deal. You'd be right. In all honesty, I *was* nervous - complete with a pounding heart, sweaty palms and nausea. I'm going out to do what? Nevertheless, I knew that I wanted to enjoy my life on my terms - sober - and I couldn't expect any establishment to clear out or screen clientele for my comfort. In my head, I knew that I had nothing to be ashamed of. I wasn't the first drunk in the universe, I'd gotten the help I needed, and was back on track. That was the pep talk I gave myself, and it worked. Again, to be honest, I picked a day bound to be quieter than others (Sunday) and the time I chose (4 P.M.) gave me a certain amount of assurance that the restaurant wouldn't be packed with people. Still, I had no idea who would be there. I also knew there was nothing I could do about it. I did what I had to do: I sucked it up, walked into the Ground Round and sat down. A certain amount of chutzpah goes a long way.

Guess what? No alarms sounded, no bells rang, and the ceiling stayed put. In other words, my unease was a product of my own mind. To patrons and workers alike, I was simply one half of a middle-aged couple out for a quick bite to eat on a Sunday in early spring. One last note of honesty: no one I knew was in the restaurant. Naturally, that made it easier. The big question is, of course, what would I have done, had there been? The question is moot. But, I believe I would have done nothing different. I'm smart enough to know that I would have drawn lots of attention, not to mention curiosity, if I had walked in, and promptly turned tail and run. Besides, I was hungry . I think you'll find as I did, that once you've broken the barrier so to speak, each time will be easier. At some point (earlier than you would have thought possible) there will be no anxiety, only anticipation of a good meal and a great time. Just like a "normal" person!

One more thing. What do you do when the item you want to order is prepared with alcohol, as indicated on the menu? You have choices – that's the beauty of a restaurant! First of all, remember that the alcohol is burned off during cooking, so that all you're left with is the taste. If that's a problem, ask if the item can be prepared without it. If it can't, order something else. The other is your favorite? Find a new one! Choices, remember? Also remember, if this is the most difficult scenario facing you in recovery, count your blessings. It could be a lot worse. In fact, come to think of it, it was.

One final note. A tribute, of sorts, to my husband and son; perhaps, also to me. On Mother's Day, a scant three months into sobriety, my husband and son took our daughter-in-law and me out for dinner. I had already "broken the ice" in a restaurant, so that wasn't really an issue. I was curious, however, to see what they would do, when the waitress asked if we wanted a cocktail before dinner. On previous occasions out (though there hadn't been many), Ron had simply ordered a soft drink, although I had assured him that if he wanted a beer, to go ahead and have one. This time might be different. He had a "partner".

To my pleasant surprise, both he and our son ordered a beer, as naturally as they had in years past. When she got to me, I asked for my usual (V.M.). The only indication that something was different was the quiet smile and almost imperceptible wink from my son, when the drinks arrived. That, more than anything, signaled for me a silent acknowledgment that the past had been put to rest. Indeed, while physically still a bit shaky, I was solid in my determination to continue my life anew as a stronger, healthier woman. That was my Mother's Day gift to them.

Be my guest

Even though you will probably be a guest in a home before you experience a restaurant, this is going to be so much easier for EVERYONE, that I decided to let it ride until now. There might be an occasion where you'll be invited into a home where the host/ess doesn't know that you've begun living a different life-style. But, I doubt it. That's why it's easy.

Your real friends, (and they're the only ones you want to see anyway) are going to be so happy that you're well and out in circulation again, they'll bend over backwards to help make you feel welcome and comfortable. They may or may not serve booze. It isn't up to you – it's not your home. If they're true friends, they'll have several choices for everyone to pick from. Word to the wise: ANYONE who offers you or encourages you to celebrate your "homecoming" with so much as one sip of alcohol, isn't a friend. They may have thought they knew you before; it's for darn sure they don't know you now, and they definitely don't have your best interests at heart. So, who needs'em?

One of the things I found to be remarkable was, before as an adult, alcohol wasn't only accepted as a natural part of social intercourse, it was expected. I had been raised to believe that was what set a "big people's party" apart from a "little people's party". If any myth could implode, that one should. I've been to all kinds of parties and social gatherings - some with booze (actually, most) and some without. Some of the guests chose to partake of alcohol, some did not. That didn't make it a party. The blending of people, the mix of personalities, the spice of different temperaments and the charged atmosphere from great conversation, *that* made it a party!

So, New Years Eve, anniversaries, birthdays? No beer? No wine? No champagne? No problem. Raise a glass of: pop, water, juice or milk – it's the toast not the taste, silly.

The important thing here, is that you're alive and starting to enjoy living again. Your friends are your friends - nothing will change that . The ones that may fall by the wayside, you don't need anyway. Just think of all of the new people you are going to meet; out of that crop, you're bound to meet at least a few roses, along with a thorn or two. Live it up! God knows you've waited long enough!

Living with the buffalo

I'm not certain why I forgot to put this section in earlier. I have a hunch, though. It's common for the brain to block out unpleasant memories. And, while this may not be my worst, it definitely ranks in the top 10.

Just prior to being released from the hospital in Grand Forks, it was determined that I should continue treatment as an in-patient elsewhere. In as much as we had no insurance, the best place (financially) was the state "facility" in Jamestown. No one believed that I could function physically on my own. We proved them wrong. They felt that I would benefit by 5-6 weeks of more therapy (mental). I proved them wrong. More about that later.

In case you haven't figured out what facility I'm referring to, I'll tell you. Every state has one, the clientele is varied, and the doors to the outside are locked. Getting in is a piece of cake. It's the State Hospital for the Mentally Ill. Most people are uncomfortable when I use the full name like that, or one of the names from my childhood: nut house, loony bin. But, that's what it is- "A rose by any other name…" No point in trying to whitewash it. I wasn't there very long - five days. They were, I think, the longest five days of my life. I hated it. I couldn't wait to be sprung. Why did I agree to go in the first place? Good question. Both my husband and I were new to this. I mean, how many of you would know exactly what to do? It's a difficult time, at best. The good folks at Altru, (and they are good) managed to convince us that I needed further therapy. That's where they thought I should go. So, I did. If they only knew what *I* know about that place. But, I'm getting ahead of myself. The morning after my release from the hospital, I was bundled off to Jamestown, ND, home to Jamestown State College, the world's largest buffalo, and the State Hospital for the Mentally Ill. What a trip! What an education!

As I said before, getting in is easy. Basically, all you say is: "I want to commit myself". The rest of the "work" is done for you. Now, when I think about saying that, I can't help but believe I must have been nuts to go along with that plan in the first place. But, I did say the words. My plea: Guilty, by reason of temporary insanity.

I should point out that when one is self-committed, one is ostensibly free to spring oneself at any time. That gurgling sound you hear is me flushing another myth down the toilet. To be sure, you can get yourself released - eventually - with one teensy, weensy caveat. All doctors, therapists and nurses need to agree to let you go. If, for any reason, they don't think you're ready, you stay put. That is, of course, unless you have a knight dressed in shining armor (or, as in my case, a cowboy hat and warm winter jacket) to rescue you. More about that later. If I live to be 100, I won't forget my arrival and intake at Jamestown.

It's a series of buildings, connected by underground tunnels, situated on a hill outside of town. It's huge. OK, North Dakota huge. It doesn't look foreboding, but the mere isolation of the complex renders it so. Inside, institutional green, relieved only by vinyl chairs in various shades of 1970's earth tones. In a word - horrid. It's not anybody's fault, it's everybody's. What are we spending our tax dollars on? How can we expect anyone to get well in that environment? All right, I'm done whining. For now. After a brief physical by a nurse, who determined that I was a physically debilitated recovering alcoholic (nothing got past her), I was escorted to the women's sector for the chemically dependent. Long walk, strange noises, and infinitely green.

Four of us to a room, although only one of my bunkies was in there when I arrived. She appeared to be older than me, but it's hard to tell what age any of us in here are. We all look like hell. During my intake, I was told I could keep $20 with me on the ward; any more than that should be placed in the safe in the office. It seems that there's a small theft problem on the wards. I'll get to that in a minute. Anyhow, I was introduced to the one roomie present, who appeared to have the flu; I thought it might have been due to the green walls. I was left to my own devices to unpack, relax and wait for my husband to join me. He'd been temporarily diverted, while I settled in. Scarcely had I started putting my stuff away, when I heard a soft hissing sound. I looked around apprehensively (snakes terrify me) and realized with relief that it was my new friend desperately trying to get my attention. Poor thing had laryngitis. Frantically, she pointed to the bed adjacent to mine and began to half-whisper, half-pantomime what appeared to be a very important message. I'm pretty good at charades, so decided to play along. It went something like this:

Roomie: "Watch out for M———. She's mean; and she likes to steal.

Me: "What can she take? I don't really have anything."

Roomie: "She doesn't care. She'll take anything. Besides, like I said, she's mean. Watch your back."

I'd heard better news. Thankfully, my husband showed up just then, and we "retired to the lounge" to visit before they brought my evening meal. He left an hour or so later, promising to return in the morning, before he left for home. I didn't realize it at the time, but he had been "encouraged" to stick around for my morning session to provide support. Understatement. While waiting for my tray (the first 48 hours, inmates aren't allowed in the dining room), my other bunkie (you know, Ms. Light-Fingers), lumbered into our room. She didn't walk, stroll, or saunter.

Good thing. This was a big woman. Ms. Laryngitis was right - she did look mean. Always thinking I can make a new friend, I smiled and introduced myself. I think she responded. It was hard to tell; a sound came out, but her lips didn't move.

When the nurse brought my tray, she told me to be sure to bring it to her, so that she could determine not only that I did eat, but how much. I was used to that, having been on "Cal-Count" in the rehab. I sat down, and lifted the lid off the tray. I had long since gotten my appetite back, but I knew I'd never eat everything they'd given me - unless it was divided into three meals. I looked it over carefully - mashed potatoes, broccoli, bread and butter, plus a couple of other items and what I presumed was some sort of meat product. I later heard a comment about the "good veal we had tonight". So, that's what it was. You couldn't prove it by me. I'm a pretty smart cookie sometimes though, and I knew that if I didn't eat, big trouble would follow, and I'd be smack in the middle of it. So, I ate most of the potatoes, half of the bread, some carrot sticks, a container of Jell-o and drank my milk. Now, how to dispose of the detritus? I should mention that, unlike the rehab, where I was looked in on several times during meals, not once did anyone check on me in the day room. Well! I was taught to rely on my wits, so I did. I peeked around the corner, down the hall to the nurse's station. There everyone stood, nurses, orderlies and attendants, drinking coffee, and chatting. Perfect. Over in the corner of the lounge stood two large metal garbage cans, one marked "Cans Only", the other clearly meant for plain old garbage. I lifted the lid on the latter (I didn't want to break any rules), and quickly swept a portion of the uneaten food into the can. Let them think I couldn't *quite* clean my plate. It worked; that time and every time thereafter.

"Good for you, Patti. You did pretty well" I thought so, too.

I know what you're thinking. What happened to all that talk about doing what you have to, blah, blah, blah? I did.

In the lounge there was no end of food to snack on, available all the time. Crackers, cereal, bread (and a toaster),jellies, peanut butter, fruit, juice, milk, coffee, and always at least one kind of home-made bars or cookies or cake. I ate - all the time. Sometimes, I ate all (well, almost all) of the meals they brought. Some of it was downright tasty. The broccoli and cauliflower met the same fate, every time it showed up(too often); I filed it under "G" for garbage. I won't eat either one.

When it was time for bed, I remembered the whisperer's warning: "Beware of thieves in the night". I'd foiled the only one that concerned me. I thought. I folded my $20 into a little coin purse, and craftily hid it underneath two pillows, one of which I'd appropriated from an empty bed. M—— got ready for bed also, plopped on her ear- phones and was soon lost in her music. I settled in for sleep, when it suddenly hit me. If M—— wanted to scrounge for my money, who was going to stop her? Me? Ninety-five pounds against her two-hundred plus? Not my other bunkie; she was in worse shape than I was! Under my pillow? Who was I kidding? I knew if she wanted anything, it was hers for the taking. To disarm me, all she had to do was immobilize me. Sitting on a corner of my nightgown would take care of that. I wouldn't be able to move. Period. The more I thought about it, the funnier it got. In seconds, I was laughing . Quietly. No point in alerting her. I finally began to drift off, when I heard mumbling coming from "you know who's" bed. The mumbling became a clearly discernible monologue, that scared the hell out of me.

" I hate you. I hate you. I'm gonna kill you, Motherfucker." Over and over again, like a mantra. I couldn't remember the last time I'd been that frightened. I didn't dare move or call out for help. She'd be on me like lightning before anyone could rescue me. I didn't sleep much that night. When a nurse came in early the next morning, M—— was gone, presumably to breakfast, so I asked her: "Do you know that M—— sings in her sleep? Do you know what she's saying?"

She nonchalantly replied that yes, everyone knew. Then she left. Wait a minute! What about me? Apparently, they had a different concept of "safety first".

My first full day there proved to be at once the worst day and the best day of my life, to date. The worst: that morning, I lived the meaning of "reaching rock bottom". The best: being at rock bottom meant that it couldn't get any worse, and might even get better. Here's the way it went. My husband arrived about 8:00 A.M. and at 9, the two of us were called into a large conference room, where about 25 people were seated in a semi-circle. Each one in turn introduced herself, and then I was invited to do the same, and explain why I was there.

I stood, and opened my mouth to speak, but my throat constricted and nothing came out. I tried again. "My name is Patti. I'm an alcoholic. I don't want to live like this anymore. Please help me". By the time I'd said my name, I was crying so hard, that I could barely speak. At some point, my husband had grabbed hold of my hand; I have no recollection of him doing so. But when I sat down, my hand was held firmly in his, tucked tight against his body.

Not unkindly, they let me cry until at least for that moment, there were no more tears. I don't know how much time had passed; the whole world seemed suspended. As my sobs subsided, the appointed leader began to speak gently, but firmly and directly to me. "Patti, you've asked for help. That's why we're here. Everyone in this room is going to do whatever they can to help you. The rest is up to you". One by one, each explained what her function was, and the role she'd play in the second act of this drama, my life. Periodically, throughout the recitations, my tears reappeared. I wasn't always immediately aware that I'd resumed crying; but, my vision blurred; it was then that I realized that my face was wet.

A sorrow big and black seemed to swallow me whole. I failed to see how anyone could help me; or why they'd want to. When I looked in the mirror, I saw failure. Failure as a wife, mother, sister, daughter, friend, human being. How could I have let this happen? More to the point, what was there left, if anything, to salvage?

Finally, it ended; it was also time for Ron to leave for home. We walked to the exit together, both of us silent. What was there to say? The staff was allowing us as much time as we needed to say good-bye, but the inevitable hung over us like an impending storm. He had a long trip ahead of him; evening and the accompanying darkness comes early in the winter in North Dakota.

Determined to put the best face possible on it, I made only one request of him: That I be allowed to turn and leave first. I didn't think I could bear to see him turn his back. He agreed; we embraced. A smile seemed impossible, but I gave it my best shot. Then turning around, I squared my shoulders and began my walk back to the ward. That's when I heard it - a soft click. Do you know what is the loneliest sound you can hear? It's the quiet latch of a door, locking you away from the rest of the world.

Attempting to hold on to my dignity, I cried quietly (how many tears can a body hold?) as I made my way back to my room, past curious yet disinterested eyes. Waiting for me was Step 1 of the 12 Steps of AA. Honest assessment and personal inventory, followed by making a list of everyone I'd harmed. I had my work cut out for me. I picked up a pen, and slowly began to write. I wasn't aware of it then, but in the black pit that was my soul there flickered a tiny light that, given time, would grow brighter and illuminate the path I'd chosen.

The remaining time I spent in Jamestown was devoted to sessions with psychiatrists and other medical personnel, therapy sessions, AA meetings and free time. Most of the stay, at least in the chemical dependency unit, is fairly structured, which is intentional. There's hard work ahead, and structure helps everyone stay focused. The problem comes during free time. Those who wish to smoke can do so on supervised trips to an outdoor patio, several times a day. Each trip is about fifteen minutes in length. It was during these that I began to realize this wasn't the place for me. The supervisors ventured only as far as the door, not outside with us. To my complete amazement, on my first trip and every subsequent trip, all conversation by the inmates centered on their last drunk, where the best 2 for 1 specials were, which bar had the best happy hour, and which bar they'd hit as soon as they got out. (That would be the closest one.) It became obvious to me that all the therapy and AA sessions in the world weren't going to make an impact of any kind on most of these people. It may have had something to do with the fact that the lion's share of them was court-committed. However, I also believe that their conversations would have taken a different bent, had a nurse, or supervisor casually strolled among the clusters of people conversing. I would take it a step further by saying that it would be difficult at the least, to be focused on drinking while maintaining a conversation about something else. I don't think any of the inmates would have had the guts to talk about their next drink while still in treatment, had they thought someone was listening. I'm sure the ACLU would have something to say about this last paragraph. I wonder if any of them have ever been in a treatment facility. Even though I didn't actively partake in the conversations, I was considered "safe", because I was one of them. So much, for the cache of being one of the "in crowd".

If further evidence is necessary regarding their attitudes towards sobriety, it was clearly demonstrated during evening AA meetings, which were compulsory. *Those* meetings were a joke. The majority of the attendees sipped coffee or a soft drink and visited among themselves, rather than listen to the speakers. I found out why after the first meeting. All but a handful, literally, were going through treatment for at least the third time. Some of them were in round six or seven. Same old, same old. And all but one other person, besides myself, were court-ordered into treatment. Anybody see anything wrong with this picture?

I came to the abrupt realization that while it's possible to *frighten* or *force* someone into sobriety, it is impossible to frighten or force anybody into *maintaining* sobriety.

Out of the five days I spent at the State Hospital, I did learn of one interesting theory one evening, by a speaker during our AA meeting. As of now, it is only that; nothing more. Some science suggests that women of Northwest European extraction (particularly Scandinavian women) may be predisposed towards problems with alcohol. More study is needed, of course, but any new knowledge based on scientific fact can only help in the battle against this illness. One fact has been known for years, and that is that women process alcohol far differently than men, due in part to musculature and weight differentials. Generally speaking, men have more muscle, while women have more fat cells. I'm not a scientist, but the way it was explained to me made sense. Muscle holds water, which helps to dilute the ingested alcohol. In women, without as much muscle and therefore less water, the alcohol isn't diluted. Consequently, when it enters the bloodstream, the concentration is higher, and affects women quicker and has longer lasting effects than it does in men. Not only does this lead to inebriation more quickly, it also has a greater and faster deleterious effect on the liver. While we're focused on the unique problems of women and alcohol, this is a good place to relate some of the experiences I had with psychiatrists and therapists, during the course of my treatment.

While still at Altru, one of the people I talked with was a woman I'll call Xenia. I like the name, that's why. Initially, I didn't like *her* at all. She made me angry. Furious, actually. Eventually, I realized that had been her motive all along. In fact, during her constant "whying" and pushing, she finally stopped and said to me: "Look at you. You're so angry. Have you ever said any of this to your husband?" My initial response was to shoot back "of course, I did", but something stopped me. Then, I looked down at my hands; they were clenched in fists so tight, the skin across my knuckles was white. It came to me that while I had protested and gotten angry about bits and pieces, I had never really articulated what was at the heart of my matter. I felt duped and betrayed. At a certain point in my marriage, our focus and direction, indeed total lifestyle had undergone a tremendous shift, that would come to have reverberating repercussions for many years. For whatever reasons - fear, need to please, or a combination of these, I'd suppressed the rage that I spoke of earlier. As far as I was concerned, my husband had literally "switched horses in midstream" on me. Haltingly, at first, I began to speak about the root of my frustration. The anger spilled out of me, like pus from a sore. It was from that moment, even though darker days lie ahead, that I knew that I wouldn't drink again. There was no need to. Unloading that misery freed me in a way that nothing else could. I was finally back in charge of myself, and the direction I would take in living my life. At least, that's what I thought. I still hadn't been all the way to the pit. Jamestown, straight ahead.

I think it no accident, that it was women who helped me to address part of what lie at the base of my anger. Other female doctors or therapists with whom I spoke, whether at Altru, Jamestown or elsewhere, seemed to have a clearer grasp of those things which troubled me. More significantly, not one of them, unlike some of their male counterparts, attempted to steer me towards the Prozac Palace for the chronically depressed.

So as I said, I met with doctors of both genders. All seemed sincere in their desire to see me get well. I had a more difficult time relating to some of the males. I butted heads with one in particular. Let me say at the outset, this dedicated and compassionate professional was not purposely obtuse. He just didn't get it; at least, not from my perspective. After a number of attempts on his part to try to get me to admit I was chronically depressed, I got angry (er). Imagine that. My definition of chronic was at direct odds, it appeared, with his. Was I depressed? You bet your ass! Acutely. Not chronically. Chronic, in my mind, implies continual, debilitating depression. Ultimately, that's what it became. To suggest, however, that it had been ongoing for years was simply not true. I do believe that suppressed anger can trigger depression; I don't, however, think that they're one and the same. Yes, in the last year or so, I had been depressed - even over extended periods of time. But, during that time there were also long stretches when I did feel hope for the future, and positive about my life. In my mind, he was misdiagnosing. I told him as much. It's entirely possible that I was splitting hairs over semantics. Of course, I believe that anything is possible.

We also engaged in an interesting discussion concerning the public's attitude towards women and alcoholism. He was of the opinion that the general public's feeling towards alcoholism in general is not colored in any way by gender. While I would certainly agree that there has been an improvement in attitude and treatment of female addicts, I sharply disagree with him in his assertion that the stigma (of alcoholism) is no greater for women than it is for men. Consider: in days not too far in the past, the words alcoholic or drunk were seldom applied to women. A special word, "dipsomania" was used to describe this condition, when suffered by females. Moreover, our popular culture had a way of portraying male drunks as somewhat comical; not too swift, but harmless members of the community sometimes spoken of with humor, if not complete respect. Not so with women. Society has had a way with dealing with these miscreants. Keep them hidden away from prying eyes. Speak of them only in whispers. That denial eventually gave way to more public, but no less damning responses to the problem.

Witness the messages sent overtly (TV, radio, books and magazines) and covertly (avoidance, shunning) through our culture: Any drunk is bad enough; nothing is worse than a woman drunk. These exact words, in fact, I have often heard repeated during my lifetime. Also, it is my personal belief that even in the 21st century, there lingers a residual attitude that women addicted to pills are somehow to be seen as less an object of scorn or derision, than a woman alcoholic. I say to you now: Whether from too many pills, or too much booze, falling down is still falling down. It's long past time to lose the attitude, the stigma and the shame. Until and unless we do, all the doctors and therapists in the world won't make a damn bit of difference. The women who need the help will remain hidden. No one can treat the invisible. Therein lies the real tragedy.

Back to the State Hospital. In spite of my desolation, I did make one new friend, Barb. Like me, she was self-committed, and determined to break free of the monster this time. She was a "second-timer", and was plagued by self-doubt. I tried the best I could to bolster her esteem; talk about the blind leading the blind!

What I had gleaned, after almost three days, is that Jamestown wasn't the place for me. At that point, I understood that I had only one thing in common with them. I was surrounded by people "just like me" but I felt more isolated than ever.

Frantic friday

By Friday, I knew I had to get out of there. I began my campaign early, informing anyone who'd listen, (as well as a few who tried to escape) that I had the right to leave because of my self-committal. The powers that be appeared to agree with me, but were vague when I asked how to get the ball rolling. It was like trying to fight my way through a wall of cotton candy. By Friday night, I was beside myself as I had made little headway and one of the other patients had told me that even self-committals could be kept in, if only one doctor recommended doing so, in the "best interests of the patient". In fact, they had a lawyer on retainer to go to court if necessary, just for that purpose. That little detail had been omitted when the counselor at Altru spoke with Ron and me.

It was late evening when I finally connected with my husband. By that time, I was nearly hysterical, having called the house several times, only to get the machine. I'd also called my daughter-in-law, who had no idea where Ron was. A UND basketball game, it turned out. He'd heard the panic in my voice coming over the machine, and called me immediately. Within ten minutes or so, I was able to explain that I needed out and why. I also told him about the "exception" to the self-committal rule. He assured me that he'd be there Sunday afternoon, and that by Monday, when a doctor was available to sign the release, I'd be on my way home. That calmed me down con-

siderably. I slept better that night and the next than I had
in years! In spite of M—— crooning her "lullaby".

True to his word, Ron was there Sunday afternoon by 4
P.M. We planned my escape down to the last detail. Then,
all we had to do was wait until morning. Our plan went
like clockwork, with Ron speaking with the doctor first
and telling him that when he left for home, I'd be his traveling companion. I met with the psychiatrist next, and told
him that while I appreciated his and everyone's efforts,
Jamestown wasn't the place for me. I informed him that I
had every intention of remaining sober "on the outside",
(which was more than anyone else on my ward could say;
I didn't bother sharing that information). By 12:30 P.M.,
we were on the road. Ron wanted to stop for lunch before
we left town, but I nixed that idea. I wanted to put as
much distance between me and Stutsman County as I
could, before I'd swallow a bite!

I don't want to leave the impression that the State
Hospital is a poor facility, or that the staff is uncaring. It
most certainly is not. They do the best they can with what
they are allotted. It is a place that is woefully understaffed
and pitifully underfunded. That's part of the problem. I'm
also of the firm belief that no one can force anybody to
change behavior - court ordained or not. Read the first two
lines of the Serenity Prayer. Bye-bye, buffalo!

Exception to the rule

I know we've left Jamestown behind, but I really need to tell you about the one person there who did for me what the doctors and psychiatrists hadn't. She helped me to see that my life wasn't over; I really hadn't ruined everything. She was a former Gulf War veteran, a military nurse, respected professional, and a recovering alcoholic. Seven years sober, she knew better than all of the doctors and therapists precisely what I was feeling. She had lived it.

She found me, my third day there, in the lounge eating my lunch. In a quiet voice, she asked if she could join me. When I nodded my head yes, she sat down, and began with: "I know how bad you feel right now. It doesn't have to be forever". I said nothing, but looked at her with a fair amount of skepticism. She went on to tell me about her own experiences, and how she had turned to alcohol, like so many others including myself had, thinking it might help sort things out. She discovered, as I did later, that never works. Suddenly, I was interested. Here was a woman much like me, who had enjoyed a successful career, was respected by colleagues, and had nearly blown her life away. Here was a woman, confident, secure, sober, living a different life, and telling me I could have the same! I had not evolved enough at that point to believe her entirely, but there was a small kernel of hope that took root that day at lunch. She didn't have all of the answers; she didn't try to explain why some of us use alcohol as a crutch. She wasn't a celebrity with a fabulous tale to tell. She was an ordinary woman caught up in a web of lies and denial, who woke up one day to realize she was at a place she didn't want to be, and had become a person she no longer recognized. I don't recall her name, and I don't think it matters much. I can see her right now, as though she were in this very room with me. I think of her often; I hope she is well. I also hope she is still practicing her own brand of "medicine" It, more than anything else to that point, helped me to find the courage within to go on.

Taking care of business

Most people are familiar with the expression "Today is the first day of the rest of your life". The meaning is clear to me. Each morning, every human being should think of the coming day as a blank piece of paper. We've said or done nothing to regret, and the day lies straight ahead , full of promise and possibilities. I think this holds especially true for people in recovery. We nearly blew it. We almost didn't get to experience "the rest of your life".

With that in mind, whether or not you have a desire or need to work, you will find yourself facing a future of "So, now what?" If you choose to not work, there's always volunteering.

More than likely though, by the time you're a few months into sobriety, you're going to want to go back to work, if you haven't already done so. You'll discover, as I have, that because of your change in lifestyle, you have a tremendous change in your energy level. It's higher. This isn't rocket science. You're eating well, sleeping well, and probably getting some kind of physical exercise, whether it's at the gym, or simply going for a walk. Combined, these contribute to a higher energy level than you've experienced in years, along with a special joie de vivre that was probably missing before. That is, if you ever had much to start with. That's not to say that you won't get tired by the end of the day - you will. You're sober, not bionic! And to risk belaboring a point, it's not to say that you won't have sad or difficult days ahead. We all know better. The difference is in how you approach those days. You beat one monster back; no reason to believe you can't cope with another. You may find, as I did, that you're going to have to put yourself "back on the block", so to speak, and auction yourself to the best bidder. Notice, I didn't say the "highest bidder". You know as well as I, money doesn't guarantee happiness. Certainly we need to earn enough to live decently. But, if your job or career "before" was not fulfilling you, or no longer had meaning for you, find something else. My best advice would be to go slow. Investigate first, to see what's out there. In all likelihood, you'll have to re-think your priorities when looking for a new job. Before I go one step further, it's also key for you to determine whether you're looking for a job or a career. There's a world of difference.

I would suggest that you start with something simple - nothing terribly challenging or taxing. By the same token, don't be afraid to take on something entirely different from what you've done before. Today, it's not unusual for people to switch careers completely after spending 25-30 years doing the same thing. While we're on that subject, you'd do well to do a skills assessment. Be brutally honest. Then, find out how you can add to or improve your skills, to make your "package" more attractive to potential "buyers".

No one is ever too old to learn

There's nothing to be afraid of. We went through all that, remember? The Adult Education program in your community, the public library, and "temp" services all have the means to help you. But, you need to inquire. In the ever-changing, technologically driven world we live in, help is just a mouse click away. Don't have a computer at home? I don't either. You can access one at the library, for a very small charge. Temp services offer computer training for free. Adult Education classes charge only a nominal fee.

Here's the important thing. You got your life back, so do something with it. Don't let anything stand in your way. Up-date your skills, and then your resume. Don't let your age be a deterrent. Many prospective employers see older employees as those not only with experience, but a well-established work ethic. Younger people have their own special talents to contribute, such as greater familiarity with the technological world. These are all highly prized commodities in today's competitive market.

Now that you've updated your skills and resume, regained your physical and mental strength, you're ready to re-join the work force. There's only one small glitch. What do you want to do? If you've chosen to stay with the job you had, then most of the preceding information is extraneous. But if that isn't the case, you have some serious thinking to do. I said before, start small. This is key, because if you don't know where you want to go next in your life, working part-time allows you the flexibility to do some career investigating. So, think: book shop, gift shop, and apparel. You can also explore the service industry. Waitperson, host/ess, motel desk clerk, day care are all geared toward those who wish to be in the work force on a limited basis. Generally you'll find that you can work as much or as little as you want . You may find that what you thought would be only a part time, interim job is something that you really like and want to pursue as a permanent career. At the worst, if you hate your new occupation, you'll know what you *don't* want to do. So here's my final advice, before heading out with the classified section of the newspaper tucked under your arm: Don't automatically dismiss anything out of hand, unless you know that it would be physically impossible for you to perform the work adequately. That's the beautiful thing about career possibilities. You just never know!

Now, you've filled out the application, turned it in, and guess what? You have an interview. You know how to dress, be prompt, and carry a positive attitude. But. There probably will come some point during the interview, when the manager/employer will get into what you might think of as "dangerous territory" by asking: What would your former employer or colleagues say about you? Or, Tell me about yourself, personally. There are some who would tell you to be careful, offer no more information than necessary without lying, in order to protect yourself.

I disagree, and I'll tell you why. You knew that I would, didn't you? All of us in recovery spent a large portion of our lives being less than forthright. Had we not, we wouldn't have found ourselves in the predicament we were in, in the first place. Second, you're past that predicament now. You have nothing to be ashamed of. You've been told that, learned to say it to yourself. Now, put your money where your mouth is. Have you only been paying lip service, or do you believe that you had an *illness?* If we ever hope to break free of the shame and the stigma, the change must begin with us. Third, prospective employers look for honesty. By holding back a portion of your history, you're not committing a lie, but it is lying by omission. Earlier on, I told you that your game- playing days were over. I meant it. I don't mean to suggest that you offer up a play by play of your recovery. A simple statement, such as, "I'm a recovering alcoholic", will suffice during your brief autobiography. Most people will admire not only your decision in becoming drug-free, they will admire your courage in admitting it, as well.

Also, you may not be aware of it, but she may have had someone close to her with the same problem. Or, the manager/employer may have had to deal with her own addiction problem in the past. There are more of us than you can imagine.

Last, although I consider this to be the "least best" reason for telling about yourself, the interviewer may find out from a source other than you. She will know that you've been less than forthcoming, and may also wonder what else you've kept hidden. An employer needs to be able to trust her employees. Deceit in the beginning of any relationship is a poor foundation upon which to build that trust. That's my opinion. I should point out, however, that it's opinion based on experience.

Whether it has been to a prospective employer, new co-workers, or a new social acquaintance, never once have I ever encountered anything but a positive response. It should go without saying, I don't simply blurt something out at the beginning of a conversation, but I've found that at some point, the topic will roll around to what we "used to do", or life changes that had a profound effect on us. Again, trust your own instincts with co-workers and the like. With a prospective new boss, I think that honesty is the best policy. Until someone proves to me that's wrong, I'll stick to it.

I began my re-entry into the work-force in a small gift/card shop in a local mall. It started out to be very part-time - 15-20 hours per week. Time and events combined to turn that into to close to 40 hours per week, in just a couple of months. I loved it! Not only was I enjoying working with the public, I was learning new skills, honing some old ones and making great new friends.

Other than the manager, whom I met during my interview, the first person I met at the gift shop was a woman slightly older than I, but one to whom I could relate in a number of ways. For example, we shared a common cultural background, not only in ethnicity, but also point of reference concerning our value structure and basic beliefs. Very early on, she asked me what I had been doing before coming there, and I had a choice to make. It turned out to be the right one; make that the best one, for both of us. I told her of my history, including the alcoholism and recovery. To my amazement, alcohol was affecting her life as well, but in a far different way. Her husband suffered from the same disease as I, only he wasn't yet ready to admit it to himself, much less to her. Through the course of my working with her, we shared stories and observations. I tried, in every way I knew how, to assure her that she was in no way responsible for the disease that had overtaken her spouse. While not entirely evolved myself, of this much I am positive: No one turns anyone into an addict, except the addict - period! Her guilt seemed to overtake her at times, and it broke my heart. It's bad enough to suffer with an alcoholic, without having to shoulder the blame or responsibility for it. Throughout the two years I worked there, we were a mini-support group for each other, she and I. I continue to see her on occasion; I do not yet have the courage to ask if her husband has come to terms with his illness. He released himself from a treatment center, after one week. Although I wasn't comfortable with it, I mostly kept my doubts to myself. After all, who was I to criticize someone who had done the same thing as I? He maintained sobriety for a while; it's my hope that he continues to do so, not only for her sake, but his own as well.

While at the gift shop, on two separate occasions, I experienced what I can only believe were special gifts, or blessings, from total strangers. The first occurred just before the Christmas season, when the store was packed with wild-eyed people in search of the perfect gift. A large section had been set up with a selection of individual Christmas cards, for giving to special people, such as family, close friends, colleagues, and the like. I approached a man, fortyish by my guess, and asked if I could be of help. He turned his gaze towards me; they were the two saddest eyes I'd beheld, since gazing at my own reflection months before. To this day, I can't tell you how I knew, or why I was sure, but I was. In a quiet voice, barely above a whisper, he told me that he was looking for a special card for his mother. He was in search of one that not only expressed the sentiments of the season, but one that would express as well, the gratitude he felt towards her. We both began to look; I'd find one and show it to him, only for him shake his head "no" in frustration. He found and discarded as many as I pulled out of the rack for him. In what seemed like desperation, he turned to me and said: "You don't understand. She's stood by me through so much. I was an alcoholic; I screwed up so bad. Mom was there for me, even after I lost my wife, my kids, and my job. You don't know how bad it was".

There it was. The opportunity I'd been looking for, for months; to give something back. I couldn't have articulated exactly what I wanted to give until that very moment. Then, it became clear: Hope. That's all. But to someone in recovery, it's everything. Others had shown me how to have faith in myself again; that was something I could do for another soul, tortured and wounded in the same way I had been. I decided quickly, and touched him briefly and softly on the arm, to make sure that I had his attention. When I was positive that I did, I looked him square in the eye, and said: "Yes, I really do know". I left it at that, but permitted a small smile to creep across my face. He stared at me momentarily, and then recognition flashed in his eyes. Neither of us said a word for a minute, and then I showed him another card I'd found. This time, success. He paid for his purchase, I thanked him and wished him a good holiday season. The merest hint of a smile stole across his face as he thanked me and walked out of the store. I truly believe that a brief encounter on a blustery December day made a difference in one person's life, if only for that moment. It is my hope, that in future moments of despair or uncertainty, he will remember our brief conversation and take from it something positive to help him through. Some five months later, I had a similar encounter with another shopper. I was able to convey again, in much the same way, my understanding of "the problem". Again, there was the look of disbelief, followed by a flicker of recognition.

The irony of the two events was not lost on me. The sincerity of my desire to help heal another human being not withstanding, it was I who had received the greater gift!

I continued to work at the gift shop until the spring of 2000. I treasure the time I spent there and the knowledge I gained. I treasure more the people I got to know, colleagues as well as the shopping public. I expected to learn more about retailing and merchandising. What I didn't expect was to learn more about myself. One more piece of the puzzle that is me, falling in place.

Socializing after work

It's common in the work world to get together with colleagues when the day has ended, for a little liquid libation. This could be seen as a "booby trap", but it doesn't have to be. Simply be aware that unlike gatherings with family and close friends, these present a greater temptation. It's not that your colleagues might undermine you; you might undermine yourself. The issue is: Are you committed to sobriety? You already know the answer to that. You didn't go through the hell you did, only to blow it, because of what others are doing. You've already discovered that you can enjoy social situations without booze, so the second question is, why start again?

My colleagues at work knew beforehand that I was a recovering alcoholic. They still asked me to join them for Happy Hour on Friday. I admit to feeling a little odd the first time we ordered our drinks. Mine was the only non-alcoholic beverage on the ticket. I was the only one who seemed to notice; the "oddity" was in *my* head, not in anyone else's. They were more concerned with the canapé tray. I finally got it! They don't find it odd; why should I? From that point on, and during all subsequent trips to our Friday oasis, we were just a group of co-workers out for friendly conversation and relaxation, after a long work-week. Lesson learned: Don't be your own worst enemy; don't look for problems, where none exist.

To celebrate or not?

As my one- year anniversary of sobriety neared, my husband began making party "noises". I had long known that of all the things I didn't want, it was a party to celebrate my lifestyle change. On the other hand, I realized what Ron was trying to do: Assure me again that he was proud of me, and that he considered my accomplishment worthy of celebration. This presented, as the British are wont to say "a sticky wicket". What to do?

I decided to be open and honest with him; we had been evolving as a couple, and were communicating better than we had for years. It turned out to be the best decision, for both of us. The next time he mentioned my approaching anniversary, I took it as an opportunity to tell him how I felt. I knew his intentions were the best; I wanted him to understand why I didn't want a big to-do. I began by acknowledging the encroaching date, and casually remarked that I knew exactly how I wanted to mark the occasion. With interest, he asked what I had in mind. What I wanted was just the two of us together, enjoying a quiet dinner, good conversation, and absolutely nothing else. He glanced at me in surprise, and then asked if I was sure that was all I wanted to do. It was my turn to assure him, and I did. That, by the way, is precisely what happened and it turned out to be one of the best evenings we have ever spent. That is how *I* chose to spend *my* anniversary. You may have other ideas. There is no wrong way or right way to observe, or not observe for that matter, this special time. As unique individuals, each of us brings a different set of feelings to the table. I know of some, who each year mark the event with a special activity of some kind. AA has its own method of marking time: so many weeks, months, and years sober. This is a personal issue, and this is my personal belief: If we are to put the past in the past and keep it there, I don't know that it's necessary to celebrate, period. To carry it further, I believe we must keep looking to the future; I said it earlier, and I think it's worth repeating: You don't want to turn into a pillar of salt. We know what we were; we aren't any longer. I, for one, don't need to be reminded of what once was. Tucked away, in the inner most recesses of my brain, is the knowledge of what used to be. It can stay there!

There is, of course, the argument that across time and cultures, there has been and continues to be, the habit of celebrating the release from any sort of bondage. To those who adhere to that precept, I would say - Go ahead, no one is stopping you. It isn't for me. At least, not the type of public celebration that comes to most people's minds.

I'm also aware of Santayana's admonition: Those who forget the past are condemned to repeat it. In all but this instance, I agree with him. In the first place, not celebrating is not the same as forgetting. Anyone who was reached through treatment will not forget. Those who fall victim to recidivism, do so not from forgetting; you need to learn the lesson before you can forget it. They didn't.

I refuse to end a chapter on celebration on such a negative note, so I also have this to say: Let every day of your life be a celebration of sorts. You don't need to look very far, to find a reason to celebrate; if you were breathing when you opened your eyes this morning, and you were aware of your surroundings, that's a reason right there. As the day progresses, there'll be others. I've found, and sometimes still do, that it's so easy to play the "why me" game. To be brutally frank, why not you? Not any one of us has to hunt very long or very far to find another human being who is suffering, and in need. To take that a step further, no one has a lock on a perfect existence. So, rather than whine about what isn't there, be grateful for what is. Celebrate that. Every day. Then, if you're still down in the dumps, have I got an idea for you. Take a run up to the children's ward of the hospital, and go for a nice long stroll. Get a good look, absorb it all. Then, remind yourself how tough your life is. Or, you can try to do something for someone else. Isn't that a great segue into the next chapter?

Giving Back

Sobriety you'll discover, if you haven't already, colors your world just as drinking did. The difference is in the tones and hues.

When I was abusing, the world was essentially a black place. Few other colors (I know, purists, black is the mixture of all color) entered in, and when they did, it was for a very brief period of time. That's not to say, by any means, that I was or that you'll be issued a pair of rose-colored glasses upon release from treatment.

Rather, sober you'll find yourself noticing, then appreciating the subtle shadings life has to offer. The world isn't perfect; nor is it a hell-hole. It just is; if you want, you have the ability to make it a friendlier place for someone else, help her to see what you see - a world filled with possibilities.

I discovered that I had a need to give back in some way, to the community at large. I believe that to be a natural extension of feeling good about yourself, and realizing that as a human being you have something of value to contribute. After some thought, I determined that inasmuch as I had received such excellent care at the hospital, I would try to give back to them, in the one way I could think of. It needed to be something that I could do before or after work. Our blood bank, like most others, was constantly on the search for donors, and frequently their supply dwindled to a frighteningly low level.

It's not as easy as you think, giving blood. It ought to be - God knows in our community at least, they have monthly "come ons", to induce a greater number of donations. I called in June, six months after my release, to make an appointment. Earlier that spring, a complete liver and blood work-up had determined that I was healthy. Unbelievably, to my doctors and myself alike, there was no discernible damage - think cirrhosis - my liver was the size it was supposed to be. Hallelujah!

After answering a few questions over the phone, almost as an afterthought, the technician inquired about my weight.

"You do weigh 110#, don't you?" What business is it of hers, how much I weigh, I thought. Thankfully, I didn't do my thinking out loud. "Well, no". "Sorry, we can't use you, unless you weigh at least 110. " You must be kidding! I'm healthy as a horse. I just got a clean bill of health from my doctor". "Sorry. If you don't weigh 110, you can't donate". Who makes up these rules? A cynic might think that any-one with viral pneumonia, but weighing 110# *would* be an acceptable candidate. It's a good thing I'm not a cynic.
I know that these places need rules, for the protection of everyone. But – doesn't it make sense to consider the whole person, and not an arbitrary number, when deter-mining who should give blood? It seems to me that they're eliminating a large segment of the population by insisting on an arbitrary weight. What about short, smaller boned people, perfectly healthy people, who weigh 100, or even 95? Talk about cutting off your nose to spite your face.
Pardon my snit. I have a small streak of rebel running through me. I am a child of the '60's. Anyway, I digress. I finally did reach their desired weight. I do donate blood regularly. They seem to find it necessary to weigh me peri-odically. I always pass.

You may decide to go another route. If your don't like needles, I highly recommend that you do. Everyday, on community bill boards in grocery stores, discount stores, TV, radio and newspapers, there's a call for help. Your help. It takes nothing but a little time from your life; it will richly enhance another's. Added bonus: it will do the same for yours.

Finding your own forgiveness

If, by the time you've gotten this far, and haven't yet realized that nothing you do or say will make any difference in your life or anyone else's until you forgive yourself, then one of us has failed. I don't like to fail; let me try again.

You will probably find, as I did, that family and friends alike will tell you "It's all right". "Don't worry about it. You're better now". "It's over. Everybody makes mistakes". All of those things are true. Nevertheless, initially I found that looking at myself, without feeling contempt, was impossible. It was also impossible to get through the day - even the early morning - without looking at myself. Washing, brushing my teeth, putting on make-up, doing my hair, all required that I spend some time looking at my reflection. Aside from the physical aftermath of what I'd put my body through, it was the embarrassment and pain reflected in my eyes, that made me turn my head. It wasn't for myself that I felt so awful. Knowing that I had caused heartache and worry for the people who knew and loved me and who I loved in return, sent me spinning into a pit I thought I'd never climb out of. I told myself I had an illness. I told myself that genetics might have had something to do with it. I told myself that I had found the courage to face the demons and win. In short, I told myself all of the things that the doctors and psychiatrists had told me. It didn't do much good. Every time I heard anyone say:

"I'm so proud of you", "We're proud of you and happy for you", I wanted to scream myself hoarse. Happy? That was somewhat more understandable. After all, I was no longer in the grips of alcohol. Proud? Of what? I felt no pride. I still felt shame. Then, I met Betty.

I had promised the shrink in Jamestown that I would see a mental health professional when I got back to Grand Forks. I made an appointment at one of the mental health centers in town, and on the appointed day made my appearance. I was ushered into the office of a woman about my age. She stood to shake my hand, and offered me a cup of coffee. She asked after my general health, and asked me how I was doing in the sobriety department. I told her so far, so good. We got to talking about life in general, and the stressors that seem to pop up around every corner. She asked me about my family - nuclear and extended. Whether it was she, the timing, or a combination of the two, I opened up to her in a way I hadn't before, to anyone. She listened without making many comments, occasionally stopping me to clarify something I'd said. At the end of my monologue, she asked me one question: "When you reached adulthood, married, started a family and a career, was it your intent to "make a mess of things?" (Those were my words, by the way.) I looked at her like she was crazy, and said that of course it wasn't. She followed the first question with another: "Did you try to do the best that you could under the circumstances?" I said that of course I did. She smiled a slow smile and then said: "Why are you unwilling to forgive yourself? You weren't perfect. Far from it. But then, no one is. You tried. You did what you thought was the best. It turns out that it wasn't. No one has any right to expect any more from you than that. Not a spouse, not your children, not siblings, parents, family or friends. You're a human being. Human beings make mistakes. This wasn't your first. It won't be your last - even sober. Think about the positive impact you've made in other areas. Think of the good that you've done. Everybody has. You've simply forgotten".

Why those words, at that moment sank in, I have no idea. I'd be lying if I said that I left there, went home, and my self-esteem blossomed. It didn't. It did, however, take root.

As I fixed lunch, I thought about some of the good times. Over the next several months, I applied that same exercise, many times, in different circumstances. Very slowly, I began to realize that I had in fact done good things, as well as bad. I had value; I was competent. I was no different than any other person on the planet. Not earth-shattering news to the average human being perhaps. To a recovering addict, it's that nourishment of the self, that is most required if recovery is to be successful. Isn't that the whole point?

The rest of your life—part deux

Life would be easy, if living it weren't so difficult. When you're through scratching your head, and wondering what lunatic came up with that bit of wisdom, I'll try to explain what I think it means.

Basically, through my journey I've discovered one simple truth: Life is pretty straightforward. *We* supply the hairpin curves. Essentially, we need air, water, food and shelter; we also need peace of mind. That's all we *need* to live. Trouble comes when we allow our wants to over-shadow our needs. There's not a thing wrong with wants, so long as they don't get in the way of what should be our priorities. Certainly, there are some wants that are as worthy as our needs, and deserve our attention. Cures for cancer, aids, diabetes and other life-threatening diseases. And, of course, world peace and greater understanding among people of all cultures and religions.

But, if you read Robert Fulgham's book, <u>All I Really Need to Know I Learned in Kindergarten</u>, you already know what you need to live your life. Focus on what's really important. *Integrity. Honesty. Kindness. Joy in simple things.* I try to. We all get side-tracked. I do that, too. Those of us who fell into the black hole, wound up there, because we lost focus of who we are and what we're about. Prioritize and focus. If we do that, we'll find peace. When we find peace, maintaining sobriety will follow.

The importance of maintaining my focus and the pursuit of inner peace were brought home to me very shortly after my discharge from Jamestown. A friend and neighbor had battled cancer for about five years. She enjoyed remission for awhile, and seemed to be living her life like she always had. I've known few people in my life, with the capacity for joy that Alice lived, every day. When she lost her hair during chemo and radiation, she slapped a hat on her head, and went about her life as always. When her illness, or the effects from it, sapped her energy, she still accomplished what she set out to, pacing herself. And then, despite her spirit, and her doctor's best efforts, the cancer raged back. While I was fighting my demons, she was fighting her own. I had brought mine on by my responses to life; hers were the result of the capriciousness of... what? God? Nature? Cosmic Practical Joke?

Shortly after I returned home, Alice came to call, bearing a cake, and wishes for my good health and recovery. As bad as I looked, Alice looked worse. It didn't augur well for her future, of that I was certain. I felt sad; I was also confused. For some reason, I was still around, and my health was improving daily. That alone was a miracle. At one point, I'd been given less than a 10% chance of survival. Alice's odds were no better than mine had been. Nevertheless, we all prayed and hoped for the best. Surely, if God saw fit to keep me around, in spite of myself, He would see the logic, the necessity, in working another miracle for a woman not responsible for her disease. Wrong. In July, 1998, Alice lost her battle. I had won mine, and was left to wonder why. Then, the guilt. Overwhelming, gut-sickening guilt. And, as much as I wanted to and knew I had to, I dreaded seeing her husband, Ben. I knew that *he knew* why I'd been hospitalized. Would he slam the door in my face? Rant? Scream obscenities?

I prepared a casserole and a cake to bring to Ben's house. Family was coming. People need to eat. Honestly, I didn't know what else to do.

My knees were doing a familiar "knock" when I stepped out of my car. Ben opened the door and bade me welcome with kind words, a smile and a warm hug. Life has a way of turning topsy-turvy when we least expect it. I was there to offer comfort and support for Ben. It was he who offered me warmth and kindness. I had so much to learn about people. I still do.

I'd be lying if I said that my guilt evaporated in that moment or even that day. I struggled. Everyday for months, I struggled. Gradually, as days turned into weeks, I came to one obvious conclusion. I am here, whether I can make sense of it or not. I doubt that I'll get an explanation in this lifetime. There seems to be no point in continuing to look for one. What I can do is this: I can honor Alice and her memory, along with that of all the others who have touched and continue to touch my life, by living each day in the best way that I can. I've been given an opportunity that so many never have - a chance to get it right. Not perfect, never that. But I try. You can, too. Go ahead. What are you waiting for?

That's all I have to say. For now.

References

Grant, B. F., Harford, T. C., Dawson, D. A., Chou, P., Dufour, M., & Pickering, R. (1994). Prevalence of DSM-IV alcohol abuse and dependence, United States, 1992. Alcohol Health and Research World, 18 (3), 243-248.

Wilsnack, R. W., & Wilsnack, S. C. (Eds.) (1997). Gender and alcohol: Individual and social perspectives. New Brunswick, NJ: Rutgers University Center of Alcohol Studies.

Biographical Profile

Sharon C. Wilsnack, PH.D.

Sharon Carlson Wilsnack received her B.A. in psychology from Kansas State University, her M.A. and Ph.D. in clinical psychology from Harvard University, and studied as a Fulbright Fellow at the University of Freiburg, Federal Republic of Germany. She is presently Chester Fritz Distinguished Professor in the Department of Neuroscience, University of North Dakota School of Medicine and Health Sciences.

Dr. Wilsnack's background includes experience as a substance abuse therapist and treatment program director as well as in research and medical education. She has published extensively on issues related to substance abuse in women, and has addressed numerous national and international audiences. She is co-editor with Linda Beckman of the volume <u>Alcohol Problems in Women: Antecedents, Consequences, and Intervention</u> (New York:Guilford Press, 1984) and with Richard Wilsnack of <u>Gender and Alcohol: Individual and Social Perspectives</u> (Rutgers Center of Alcohol Studies, 1997).

Sharon Wilsnack and Richard Wilsnack direct a 20-year longitudinal study of drinking behavior in U.S. women, and coordinate and international collaborative research project on gender and alcohol which involves researchers from 35 countires. Sharon Wilsnack is a Fellow of the American Psychological Association, and served as member of the Institute of Medicine's Committee to Study Fetal Alcohol Syndrome and as a member of the National Advisory Council on Alcohol Abuse and Alcoholism of the U.S. Department of Health and Human Services. She is presently a member and panel chair of the Subcommittee on College Drinking of the National Advisory Council on

Alcohol Abuse and Alcoholism, National Institute on Alcohol Abuse and Alcoholism.

She is married to sociologist Richard Wilsnack and it the mother of five children.

Academic Appointments

1985-present: Professor and Director of Preclinical Curriculum, Division of Psychiatry and Behavioral Science, Department of Neuroscience, University of North Dakota School of Medicine and Health Sciences

1989-present: Adjunct Professor, Department of Psychology, University of North Dakota

1989-present: Chester Fritz Distinguished Professor, University of North Dakota

Other Professional Experience

Research Assistant to David C. McClelland, Department of Social Relations, Harvard University

Clinical Psychology Intern, Massachusetts Mental Health Center, Harvard Medical School, Boston

Supervising Psychologist, Massachusetts Mental Health Center, Boston

Director, Regional Alcoholism Rehabilitation Program, and Coordinator of Addiction Services, South Central

Community Mental Health Center, Bloomington, Indiana

Co-Director, Clinical Research Training Program in Alcoholism, Department of Psychology, Indiana University

1978-present: associate Director, International School of Alcohol Studies, University of North Dakota and North Dakota Division of Alcoholism and Drug Abuse

Honors and Awards

1961-present: Putnam Scholarship, Phi Kappa Phi, Mortar Board, Senior Prize in Psychology, Phi Beta Kappa Honor Senior Award, Kansas State University

1966-67: Woodrow Wilson Graduate Fellowship, Harvard University

1965-present: Biographical Listings: Who's Who in American Colleges and Universities, Outstanding Young Women of America, Who's Who in the Midwest, Who's Who of American Women, American Men and Women of Science, Who's Who in Science and Engineering, Who's Who in the World

1991: Betty Ford Lecturer, association of Medical Educators and Researchers in Substance Abuse

1995: Psychologist Lifetime Achievement Award , North Dakota Psychological Association

1999: First Annual Terry McGovern Research
Award, Terry McGovern Foundation,
Washington, DC

Consultation and Service Activities

1988-present: National Advisory Board, Women's
Alcohol and Drug Education Project,
Women's Action Alliance, New York, New
York

1988-present: Chair, Scientific Advisory Board,
Research Institute on Alcoholism (later
Research Institute on Addictions)
Buffalo, New York

1993-present: Organizer, International Research Group
on Gender and Alcohol, a component of
the Kettil Bruun Society for Social and
Epidemiological Research on Alcohol,
Krakow, Poland, June 1993 (and subsequent meetings)

1993-94: Consultant, Fetal Alcohol Syndrome
Epidemiology Project (Philip May, PI),
Center on Alcoholism, Substance Abuse
and Addictions, University of New
Mexico, Albuquerque

1994: Member, Working Group on Women in
Transition, Center for Substance Abuse
and Mental Health Services
Administration, U. S. Department of
Health and Human Services,
Washington, DC

1997-1998:   Co-Chair, Working Group on Alcohol and
               Other Drug Use, Disorders and
               Consequences Beyond Hunt Valley:

               Research on Women's Health in the 21st
               Century, conference and report sponsored
               by the Office of Research on Women's
               Health, National Institutes of Health,
               Bethesda, MD

1998-:   Consultant, St. Petersburg Women's
               Health Project, Pavlov State Medical
               University, St. Petersburg, Russia

1999-:   Member, Board of Trustee, Alcoholic
               Beverages Medical Research Foundation,
               Baltimore, MD

Editorial Activities

1974-present: Editorial Reviewer for: Journal of
               Abnormal Psychology, Journal of
               Consulting and Clinical Psychology,
               Journal of Homosexuality, Journal of
               Personality and Social Psychology,
               Journal of Studies on Alcohol, Alcohol
               Health and Research World, Social
               Problems, Alcoholism: Clinical and
               Experimental Research, Addiction, Sex
               Roles, Women's Health, Psychology of
               Women Quarterly, and others

Addresses and Workshops

Risk factors for alcohol abuse in women: Findings from a
               U.S. national

longitudinal study. Presented to research staff and interviewers of the St. Petersburg Women's Health Project, Pavlov State Medical University, St. Petersburg, Russia, February, 1999.

Women are different: Some implications for alcohol research. Invited presentation, Putting Special Populations on the Alcohol Research Agenda: A Tribute to Edith S. L. Gomberg's Work, University of Michigan Alcohol Research Center, Ann Arbor, MI, October, 1999

Twenty years of research on women and alcohol: New findings and future directions. Invited presentation, Cooper Colloquium Series, Rutgers University Center of Alcohol Studies, New Brunswick, NJ, September,2000

International research on gender and alcohol: Recent progress and some implications for alcohol policy. Plenary presentation, Scientific Conference on the Use and Misuse of Alcohol by Women, sponsored by the National public Health Institute of Sweden, Runo, Stockholm, Sweden, April 3-4, 2001